Praise for . . .

Work Like You're Showing Off!

"Joe Calloway is a show off who can back it up. Joe Calloway is not just an expert; he's a world-class expert. Joe Calloway is not just a master; he's a world-class master. Joe Calloway delivers a lesson of reality that will kick start your success. Buy his book, read his book, study his book, and implement his book so that you can achieve and show off your world-class mastery, world-class expertise, and wealth."

> —Jeffrey Gitomer
> Author, *The Little Red Book of Selling* and *The Little Gold Book of YES! Attitude*

"Joe teaches you to let go of your excuses, break out of your chains, crawl out of your rut, drop your baggage at the door, then kick the door down and grab life by the throat so you can actually become the person you most admire. I love this book! Finally, a fun, refreshing alternative to the motivational mumbo-jumbo. Instead it's an action plan for personal excellence."

> —Larry Winget
> Author, *It's Called Work for a Reason!* and *Shut Up, Stop Whining, and Get a Life*

"Show off at work? I'd never thought about it in those terms. Then Joe Calloway wrote this stimulating little book and it makes perfect sense. He explains how to show off the right way and bring your best to your work everyday, and why the biggest beneficiary isn't your employer or customer (although they'll love it), but you. So read this book, and start showing off at work. You'll be glad you did."

> —Mark Sanborn
> Author, *The Fred Factor* and *You Don't Need a Title to Be a Leader*

"*Work Like You're Showing Off!* isn't just an inspiring and practical success guide, it's the very key to personal excellence in the 21st century. And here's the bonus—it's an absolute blast to read. You're going to love this book!"

> —Steve Farber
> Author, *The Radical Edge: Stoke Your Business, Amp Your Life, and Change the World*

"Calloway always has something to say, and he's always worth listening to. His new book is straight talk on success. Read it fast!"

> —Randy Gage
> Author, *Why You're DUMB, SICK, & BROKE . . . And How to Get SMART, HEALTHY, & RICH!*

WORK LIKE YOU'RE SHOWING OFF!

WORK LIKE YOU'RE SHOWING OFF!

The Joy, Jazz, and Kick of Being Better Tomorrow than You Were Today

JOE CALLOWAY

BICENTENNIAL
1807
WILEY
2007
BICENTENNIAL

JOHN WILEY & SONS, INC.

Published by John Wiley & Sons, Inc., Hoboken, New Jersey.
Published simultaneously in Canada.

Wiley Bicentennial Logo: Richard J. Pacifico

For general information on our other products and services or for technical support, please contact our Customer Care Department within the United States at (800) 762-2974, outside the United States at (317) 572-3993 or fax (317) 572-4002.

Wiley also publishes its books in a variety of electronic formats. Some content that appears in print may not be available in electronic books. For more information about Wiley products, visit our web site at www.wiley.com.

Lyrics for "Let's Be Too Much" in Chapter 10 appear with permission from the songwriter, Rebecca Folsom.

Library of Congress Cataloging-in-Publication Data:

Calloway, Joe.
    Work like you're showing off! : the joy, jazz, and kick of being better tomorrow than you were today / Joe Calloway.
      p. cm.
      ISBN-13: 978-0-470-11626-5 (cloth)
    1. Success in business.   2. Creative ability in business.   I. Title.
    HF5386.C243   2007
    650.1—dc22

                                                              2006102356

Printed in the United States of America.

10 9 8 7 6 5 4 3 2 1

For
Catherine Jin Fu Calloway
Welcome home, little girl.

Contents

Acknowledgments   xi

1. Showing Off   1

2. Grand Stupidity and Absurd Bravery   9

3. All Hat and No Cattle   15

4. Let It Go   17

5. The Gold Standard   25

6. Get in the Damn Boat and Go   27

7. As Good as You're Going to Be   31

8. We See Things as We Are   35

9. Stupid Promises   43

10. Let's Be Too Much   47

11. Imagination Will Take You Everywhere   51

12. Get Back inside the Box   59

13. Expect to Connect   63

14. Going All In   69

15. Joe and Muhammad   75

16. We Haven't Seen That   81

17. The Pursuit of Happiness   83

18. The Enemy of Future Success   91

19. What You Think of Me Is None of
    My Business   95

20. Whatever Happens Is Normal   99

21. Guess What I Want and Other Stupid
    Mind Games   105

22. I Said I Don't Know   109

23. The Golden Circle of Ignorance   113

24. What Have You Done for Me Next?   119

25. The Power Strategy   123

26. Your Next Best Idea Is Everywhere   127

27. What Matters Most   137

Acknowledgments

Thank you to my friends, colleagues, and sources of inspiration that have helped me along the way on this most amazing ride (so far). Thanks to Matt Holt and everyone at John Wiley & Sons, Inc.; Kris Young, John Gaspard, and everyone at Martin Bastian Productions; Jane Atkinson; Lisa Yakobi; Sue Remes; Toni Newman; Larry Winget; Dale Irvin; George Campbell; Victoria LaBalme; Jeffrey Gitomer; Joy Baldridge; Lou Heckler; Lisa Ford; Mark Sanborn; Steve Farber; Chip Emerson; Randy Gage; Todd Engel; MPL; Digital Dog; Martha Kelly and the Center for Professional Development at Belmont University; Joe Scarlett; Stephanie Brackman; Jim Cunningham; Cheryl Plummer and everyone at Pinnacle Financial; Rebecca Folsom; Tom Kimmel; The Thingers; Randy Pennington; Coke Sams; Ray Waddle; Michelle Joyce; Second Presbyterian Church in Nashville; the National Speakers Association; Sting; Prince; Jerry Seinfeld; Brian Palmer; Rich Gibbons; Mary Ellen Lipinski; Mirror Restaurant; Gin Calloway; John and Sherry Calloway; Bob and Carolyn Calloway; Ellen Bush; Lawrence and Polly Alexander; and, more than I can possibly say, my daughter Jess and the light of my life, my wife, Annette.

You only live once, but if you work
it right, once is enough.

—Joe E. Lewis

WORK LIKE YOU'RE SHOWING OFF!

1

Showing Off

Showing off has been variously defined as pretentious-ness, exaggeration, posturing, bragging, inflated self-importance, arrogance, bigheadedness, pride, conceit, being full of yourself, immodesty, being vain, haughty, and overweening. Overweening? My goodness! Who, in their right mind, would want to be thought of as over-weening? The shame! The horror!

Those definitions are all misguided interpretations of what is, in fact, the most noble of pursuits. Showing off is completely misunderstood and has gotten a very bad rap. What the world needs is not less showing off, but more. If you're not showing off, then what's the point? If you're not showing off, then why even show up? Why go to work? Why play the game?

Showing off, as I define it (which I can, because this is my book), is a good thing. Showing off is about bringing the best you have to any situation. It's about excelling; exceeding expectations; and experiencing the joy, jazz, and kick of being better tomorrow than you were today. When presented with a problem or challenge, showing off is an attitude that says, "Watch this."

This book was inspired by Leslie, who works at the Kinko's on Hillsboro Road in Nashville, Tennessee, and others like her. Trying to put into words the subtle magic that Leslie works with customers is like trying to catch lightning in a bottle. I can't quite put my finger on what it is about Leslie that is so remarkable, but something about the way she does her job is so smooth and quietly wonderful that you walk away feeling a little bit better about yourself and the world.

Part of it is the gleam in her eye. Or is it a twinkle? No, I think it's a gleam. It's like there's something really cool going on and Leslie is letting you in on it. One aspect of Leslie's quiet version of showing off is that if you have a special request or unusual order, she seems to handle it so effortlessly that it's like watching Tiger Woods make a three-foot putt. It's just what Leslie does.

Then there's her sense of humor. It's always there, just below the surface. Leslie isn't someone that makes me laugh out loud with jokes. She's much better than that. I can't be around Leslie without smiling because her smile is infectious. If you're in a bad mood, I would recommend that you go see Leslie about some copies. The rest of your day will go better.

I don't know Leslie personally. I'm just one of her customers. I haven't even done business with her enough to say that we're acquaintances. But if someone told me to put together a "dream team" of people that I'd want to work with on a variety of projects, I'd pick Leslie to be on the team. Something about her says that she could handle pretty much whatever assignment you put in front of her. Like most really good show-offs, especially the subtle, classy ones, there's just "something about" Leslie.

For the true show-off, work is play. When you watch a show-off do their work, it's like watching a little kid caught up in the joy of making mud pies. Showing off means being in a state of flow in which you can almost stop thinking about what you're doing because it comes so naturally.

In a customer focus group conducted for an auto manufacturer, the participants were asked to relate an example of extraordinary service. A woman told of her experience with a hotel employee in New York who, when she told him that she had left her coat in a restaurant across town that evening, told her not to worry about a thing, that he would take a taxi to the restaurant, retrieve the coat, and bring it to her. An hour later, the same employee appeared at her hotel room door, her coat in hand, which he presented to her neatly folded and wrapped in tissue paper. That's showing off.

The beauty of showing off is that it's probably most effective when done quietly. You know who I'm talking about. It's the coworker who, without fanfare or calling attention to herself, simply gets things done. It's the guy in operations who, when faced with yet another seemingly impossible task, smiles and says, "I'll make it happen." It's the customer service representative who, when you call with a request that you know in your heart of hearts is probably unreasonable, tells you that it's her pleasure to take care of it for you. And, yes, it's the player who, when the game is on the line, says, "Give me the ball, coach."

At this point, there will be some who will claim their usual role as the "victim" and say, "Aha! I see what you're up to! You just want me to bust my butt and do extra work to make everybody else happy and make my company more money and take advantage of me!" Yeah, right. Cry me a river.

Let's get this straight. Showing off is something you do because it's first and foremost in your own best interest. Showing off is about getting what you want while having one hell of a good time doing it. Showing off is about squeezing maximum fun out of any situation, and having the brains, guts, and creativity to not only make lemonade when life throws you lemons, but also make a lemon meringue pie, a lemon cake with festive lemon icing rosettes, and a lemon "watch this" soufflé.

The wonderful by-product of showing off is that you bring maximum value to what you're doing for whomever you're doing it. The bottom line on how the world works most of the time is that the best way to get what you want is to be sure the other person is getting what they want. If you don't understand that, then you don't understand the basic fundamental operating principles of business, relationships, politics, or playground dynamics.

Showing off means finding the best way to win—which requires you to find the best way to let the other person win, too. If you doubt that this is true, I invite you to try the strategy of making the other guy lose. Do it. Make sure that whoever you're playing with loses, whether it's your coworker, spouse, child, friend, customer, vendor, or the ticket agent at the airport when your flight has just been cancelled. Go for it. Make that person lose. Then see what happens, Mr. or Ms. Tough Guy.

They won't play with you anymore. That's how it works. If you make people lose, aren't fun to play with, or are just generally a pain in the ass to be around, people will stop playing with you. They will pick up their ball and go home.

Showing off means that when the easy route would be to get mad, be unreasonable, or generally raise hell about whatever perceived injustice is taking place (e.g., the cancelled flight), you completely surprise everyone and remain the coolest person in the room. You handle it. You are the oasis in the desert, the calm in the storm, the cooling rain in the firestorm of raging insanity. When everyone else is screaming bloody murder at the airline ticket agent, you tell him that he's doing a good job, to hang in there, that this, too, shall pass. Then watch when the ticket agent puts you at the head of the list for the next flight. That's showing off.

If you think that's not the way it works, you're so dead wrong that I can't even find the words to adequately describe it. The idea of winning through intimidation is a myth perpetuated by losers who are bitter about their own lives. Stop screaming and start showing off. Do it quietly and with class. It's magic. It's jaw-droppingly amazing in its effectiveness. Showing off under pressure is elegant. It's a beautiful thing.

Don't think for one second that I'm saying you should be a wimp and let people walk all over you. To the contrary, show-offs never, ever, ever let anyone take advantage of them or have their rights trampled by a bully. It's just that show-offs pick their battles wisely. They use their heads. They're tough, but they're smart.

If I haven't yet won you over to this new way of thinking about showing off, I can only invite you to read on. There are ideas in this book that will, I hope, challenge your beliefs about lots of things. I'm writing this book to be provocative, not pleasant. For many people, maybe even for most people, understanding this completely positive interpretation of showing off takes a little getting used to.

When I told my friend Joy Baldridge the title of this book, she was her usual diplomatic self with her feedback. She said, "I hate it. I don't like anything about it. I don't like show-offs and I don't like this title." Did I mention that Joy is my friend and therefore feels she has an obligation to be completely honest with me? Did I also mention that Joy is a woman who teaches people how to be more productive while reducing stress? And did I further mention that she is one of the most delightfully outrageous show-offs I have ever known?

Joy does wildly creative live presentations before audiences all across the country. When I watch her work, I wonder how on earth she comes up with the courage to get on stage and do the completely insane things that she does. Doesn't she know the rules? Doesn't she know that that's just not the way it's done? And why do her audiences squeal with such absolute delight? Why do they so adore what she does for them and the value that she brings to them in her own totally unique, off-the-wall, outside-the-box way?

Because she's showing off, that's why. Joy has decided to hell with the way it's always been done. Let's not play it safe. Let's do something meaningful, and let's do it in a way that's fun, inspiring, and amazing. People love her for it.

When I pointed this out to my friend Joy, she said, "Oh, you mean THAT kind of showing off! You mean showing off in the sense of 'You go, girl!' You mean showing off as in being your very best by doing what you do better than anybody else. You mean showing off in the way that you're bringing something to the table that makes other people happy and helps them and really contributes to the world!"

Well, yeah. That's exactly what I mean. Whether it's over the top or so quiet and understated that you hardly even notice it, showing off is about making a positive contribution.

By the way, Joy's logo is a silhouette of herself jumping with wild abandon (jumping for Joy—get it?). It inspired the cover of this book. That Joy. What a show-off. We need more. Keep reading.

2

Grand Stupidity and Absurd Bravery

There's something that you've wanted to do for a long time, isn't there? It's been simmering there in the back of your mind. You think about it at night sometimes as you go to sleep. It might be a book that you want to write, a marathon that you want to run, a move to another country, or a business you want to start. It could be anything; whatever it is, the thought gets you going. It energizes you. But you haven't done anything about it yet because you know what people will say.

People will tell you that your idea is ridiculous. People will tell you that you don't know enough; that it won't work; that no one's ever done it before; or that you're just dreaming. They'll tell you it's not practical, possible, or realistic. They'll tell you that you'll mess it up, lose every-thing, or are making a huge mistake. They'll tell you that you aren't trained in that, haven't done it before, or don't have enough experience.

Casey Stengel once said, "They say you can't do it but that doesn't always work." He's right. Here's another blinding flash of the obvious: 100 percent of the things you don't try, won't happen.

It's all well and good to listen to your friends' advice and counsel, but sometimes you just have to take it all in and then say, "To hell with it. I'm doing it anyway." Let go of what they think and listen to what you think.

If you wait until everything's perfect, it won't happen. If you wait until you know everything you're supposed to know, it won't happen. If you wait until it's a sure thing with no chance of failure, it won't happen. Do it now, or it may never happen.

Some say that the advantage of experience is in know-ing what works. But the great disadvantage of experience is the loss of the grand stupidity and absurd bravery that comes with not knowing what works. Because when you don't know what works, you'll try anything. You'll be too ignorant to play it safe. You'll be ridiculous and auda-cious. You'll discover all the new things that work. And you'll have all the fun.

There's nothing wrong with making plans or having goals. They give you direction, motivation, and a sense of order, which are all good things. The potential problem with plans is that we can fall in love with the planning and never get to the doing. Besides, no matter how well thought out your plans are, once you get going, they'll have to change. Remember the old saying, "If you want to make God laugh, tell him your plans." The point is to not get too tied to any preconceived notion about how you think things are going to turn out. If life is good at anything, it's good at throwing us curveballs.

One of the most insidious traps we can fall into is the trap of wanting to be sure that everything's going to work perfectly before we try it. We want to know exactly what the outcome is going to be before we make a move. That's what freezes us. We want all the answers when the answers aren't available.

Join me in a brief visualization exercise. Imagine you have spent six weeks climbing a mountain to get to the wise guru who lives alone at the icy summit. This guru is the master who knows the meaning of life and the answers to all questions. Your conversation goes something like this:

Oh great and all-knowing guru, what is the meaning of life?

Life is doing stuff. As opposed to death, which is not doing stuff.

Okay. That's out of the way. Now I have a couple of specific questions.

Fire at will, babe. That's why I'm here.

Is the stock market going to go up or down?

Both. I just don't know when it's going to do which. You play your money and you take your chance.

Can you be okay with that? If not, stay out of the stock market. Because nobody knows. If you're going to make money in the stock market, you have to let go of needing to know what's going to happen next. The best you can do is make a good guess.

Okay, let's change the subject. I'm thinking about going on a Caribbean cruise this summer. Will the weather be nice?

Who can say? The weather will be weather. You're asking the wrong question. Try again.

Okay. If I go on a Caribbean cruise this summer, will it rain?

Wrong question. Try again.

Okay. If I go on a Caribbean cruise this summer, will there be at least 90 percent sunshine?

Not at night. You bore me. Stop wasting my time asking me the wrong questions. Ask the right question or get off the mountain.

Okay. If I go on a Caribbean cruise this summer, will I have fun?

Bingo. Give the tourist a cigar. That's the right question. So, will you have fun?

That's what I asked you.

And it's the right question. Will you have fun?

I don't know. That's the question.

I know. And it's the right question. And my answer is, will you have fun?

Stop it. You're avoiding answering the question. You're a lousy excuse for a guru.

Don't be such a drama queen. You're just getting irritated because you climbed all this way and now you're dealing with concepts that are beyond you.

What concepts?

Like the concept that you have to let go of whether it rains or snows or sleets or hails on your Caribbean cruise. "Not raining" isn't always available. But "having fun" is almost always available. Worst scenario is it rains. Hey, ever heard of an indoor toga party? Ever heard of a having a limbo contest in the rain? Ever heard of curling up in your cabin with a good book, or a good movie, or a good shipmate and listening to the rain beat on the ship while you toss gently on the waves?

So, your point is that there's no guarantee?

Not about weather. About fun, yes. You can guarantee it yourself. It's about options, pal. Create options. Be flexible. People and the weather, sheesh. You get all upset about such small issues. You let tiny details ruin your day. Loosen up. Be okay with not knowing.

But I thought that you knew everything.

I know that I don't know. Therefore, I know.

What?

Never mind. What I do know is that if you can't have fun unless everything suits you, you are no party animal.

So what should I aspire to?

To be a fun hog. But to be a fun hog you have to be okay with not knowing what's going to happen. Fun hogs are, above all, flexible. Fun hogs can let go of what they were hoping would happen. Fun hogs can roll with what *is* happening. Let go of certainty. Embrace uncertainty. It's way more fun.

Let's do another little mental exercise. Imagine that I'm your doctor, and I say to you: "You're going to die. You have a condition that is incurable. You have a limited amount of time left. The frustrating thing about this condition is that I can't tell you exactly how much time you have. You might be dead before I finish this sentence. You might die in a week. Or a month. Or you might live to a ripe old age. There's just no way to tell. But you are going to die."

Which, of course, you are. We all are. You may be frustrated or even angry with me for telling you this. You may say, "Well that's just great! Thanks for the news bulletin! I'm going to die! So exactly what am I supposed to do with that information, Doc?"

Good question. So exactly what *are* you supposed to do with that information? Maybe it's time for some grand stupidity and absurd bravery. When you die, your biggest regrets won't be about what you did. They'll be about what you did not do.

Get stupid. Get absurd. Get busy. Show off.

3

All Hat and No Cattle

Why should I do business with you instead of your competitor? Why should I hire you instead of the other guy? Why should you get the promotion instead of your coworker? You say because you're the best choice. Fine. But don't tell me. Show me. Prove it. Put up or shut up.

What are you willing or able to do that the other guy isn't willing or able to do? What do you know that your competition doesn't know? Do you have information that they don't have? Do you perform a service that they don't perform? Do you have skills that they don't possess? Maybe your differentiator is your incredible attitude. That's fine. I can choose you based on any of those differentiators. But prove it.

In the movie *Jerry Maguire*, the great line that everyone remembers is "Show me the money!" Don't tell me what a great job you'll do. Prove it. Show me the money. Stop promising and start delivering. Jerry Seinfeld once said that after he ended his phenomenally successful television show, whenever he performed live he had about five minutes of grace from an audience. They'd give him that simply because he was the famous Jerry Seinfeld. But after that five minutes, he had to be funny. Nobody cared how funny his television show used to be because they were sitting in a nightclub or concert hall and had paid their money to be entertained. He had to deliver the goods.

We've all had the experience of knowing or working with someone who talks a good game. I once saw a sales representative for a major telecommunications firm completely charm one of his company's senior executives with some most impressive dinner conversation about the art of selling. The executive made a favorable comment about this conversation to the rep's manager, who responded that the guy could talk a great game, but that he couldn't sell his way out of a paper bag. In Texas, they call that "All hat and no cattle."

The operative word in show-off is "show." Braggarts talk about it. Show-offs do it. Hey, you may be the greatest thing since the wheel, sliced bread, and Aerosmith. So show me. Prove it.

4

Let It Go

Let it go. This is an elementary truth. The understanding of this truth is the beginning of what can change your work and life forever. If you don't have what you want, it's probably because you haven't yet let go of something that's in your way. Something in your life is taking up space. Right now, as you read these words, you already know what it is, don't you? If not, read on. It will begin to reveal itself. Pay attention when it does because letting it go may be your most important work. Showing off starts with letting go.

We live in a society obsessed with getting. We believe that by getting we can be happy and so that's what we focus on. In fact, the key to happiness, productivity, fulfillment, joy, peace of mind, and success by almost any definition is to first let go. Release what's getting in your way. It's the release that creates the space for what you want to come in naturally. Life is short. We need to get on with it.

Consider yourself warned. Letting go is a very scary thing to do. Letting go will test you like nothing ever has. You have to be courageous to let go of what's holding you back. It will be incredibly hard. It will push every button you've got. Letting go is an adult dose of reality. And sometimes reality bites. Hard. This is as in-your-face confrontational as it gets, but it will set you free.

It can be absolutely terrifying to let go of the limits, barriers, and obstacles that keep you from living the life you say you want. That's because you love those limits so very much. You lean on them. You count on them. You're used to the barriers. You're comfortable with the obstacles. Oh sure, you complain and moan and groan about them, but admit it, you've become very attached to them. All those things in your life that keep you from getting what you really want are the very things that you cling to as if they were as essential to you as the air that you breathe.

As someone who has worked for over a quarter of a century with corporate clients in every field of business that you can imagine, let me assure you that the same idea goes for entire companies and organizations. It's called *corporate culture*. Most corporate cultures, without realizing it, embrace self-limitation. Cultures of holding on to the way things have always done can be incredibly entrenched. Letting go is even harder for companies than it is for individuals.

The thoughts, habits, attitudes, and strategies that you need to let go of are wicked, insidious demons. They work their way under your skin and into your life until they become part of the very fabric of your existence. On some level, either conscious or subconscious, you are as familiar with what you need to let go of as you are with the back of your hand. At some point while reading this, you may very well stop, look up, and think, "I know what I need to let go of." It's been right there with you all the time.

The way life works is that you cannot catch the next thing unless you open your hands and let go of what you're holding now. Before you can add something that you want, you have to clear the space. You can't steal second base unless you're willing to take your foot off first base. The harbor is safe, but you'll never discover new worlds if you don't leave it. You can't climb the ladder unless you take your foot off the rung that you're on. The metaphors and clichés go on and on until they become nauseatingly overwhelming in their truth and logic.

Some people define themselves not by what they aspire to, but by what holds them back. For you, it might be a past failure that has convinced you that you can never experience significant success. Or maybe you suffered shame or heartache in a relationship that now haunts every friendship or romance that you have. Too often we think, "I failed once, therefore I will always fail." Or we think, "I succeeded by doing it this way before, therefore I must always do it this way." Either way you're in a rut, and a rut is a grave with the ends knocked out.

Thinking about letting go can be confusing and frustrating. That's because what you need to let go of may be the exact opposite of what someone else needs to let go of. You may be frozen by inaction and uncertainty. You may not be achieving what you want because you won't make a move unless everything's perfect. I, however, may not be accomplishing my goals because I an acting in a thousand different directions at once. I may need to let go of constant activity so that I can create the space for peace and quiet to enter my life and calm me down. You may be stuck in not doing anything, and I may be stuck in doing too much. You may need to hit the ground running. I may need to lie down and take a nap.

You may need to let go of suffering in silence. You might have been pushed around by someone for years and you're tired of putting up with it. Good for you. Let go of your inaction. Raise whatever hell you need to raise in order to protect yourself. It could very well be that you've always cast yourself in the role of the powerless victim. Let it go. Stand up for yourself.

You may need to let go of a place. Where should you live? Where you are now or somewhere else? As The Clash so succinctly put it, "Should I stay or should I go?" Let go of where you are now and move. Or let go of thinking that you have to be somewhere else. The answer for you may be to accept where you are. There's a wonderful bit of Zen wisdom that says, "If you want to know where you're supposed to be, look at your feet." Even if you wish with all your heart that you could just disappear from this place, this world, this life and be somewhere else, it could be that you are exactly where you are supposed to be. This may be exactly where you need to be to learn whatever lesson it is you need to learn from whomever it is that you need to learn it from.

You may find it frustrating that, while telling you that letting go is essential to your happiness and well-being, I'm not telling you specifically what to let go of or giving you an easy to follow five-step "how-to-let-go" plan. Forget it. There's no plan. There's no magic formula. There's no paint-by-numbers guide to follow. If you need, for example, to let go of certain people in your life, then you have to figure out how to make that happen. Quit calling them. Stop rescuing them. I don't know. You figure it out. It's different for everyone and for every situation. The big, blinding flash is to realize what or who it is that you need to let go of. Once you do that, you'll know how to make it happen. Trust yourself. You will know what to do. Whether or not you choose to do it is another matter entirely.

So what is it that you should let go of? Maybe it's worry, or bitterness, or anger, or envy. It could be that you need to let go of doing your work the way you've always done it while expecting a different result. For many people, the great liberating moment of their lives comes when they realize that they need to let go of everybody else's idea of success. You may experience a blinding flash of "To hell with them and what they think." Bingo. How cool is that? Can you imagine the freedom that comes with letting go of what "they" think you should want and working instead from a clean canvas of possibilities?

However, it could be that your path to peace and ful-fillment is to take the spotlight off yourself and put it on the other people in your life. Try giving instead of getting. See if you can possibly pry your clenched fingers off some of your money and give it away for a change. Give your time away. Help someone else get what they want. Your heart might fill up and your joy might come back. I don't know. But you know, don't you?

Letting go is like almost everything else. It's not what we don't know that hurts us. It's what we know and don't do that does the damage. Just know that your liberation and your success will begin with what you are willing and able to let go of. You begin to realize your greatness and experience true freedom as you open up space by letting go. The amazing thing is that by letting go, you may find that you don't particularly need goals at all. When you eliminate the negative in your life, it tends to be replaced by the positive. You don't necessarily have to conjure up anything in particular, just open up and let the good stuff flow in.

You may be one of those people who devote a lot of time and energy to goal setting. You get up every morn-ing and recite your list of affirmations. You look at the photographs in your dream book. You want to live your life like it was right off the pages of your favorite maga-zine. Your focus is directed outward at everything that you want and you have a clear vision of how you'd like your life to be. And you wonder why it's not happening. Why aren't all those things coming into you life?

Turn around and face the other direction. Stop focusing on what you want to get, or own, or achieve. Look within yourself. The only way any of those things you aspire to will ever make an appearance is if there's room for them. The great truth for you may very well be to let go of those things you thought you wanted. When you look deeply enough, you may discover that you didn't want them at all. This can be liberating and painful at the same time. The liberation of being released from the slavery of, for example, killing yourself and your spirit by scratching and clawing your way up some ladder of success may very well be accompanied by the temporary pain of letting go of that dream. Be patient. Clear the space. That's the first step.

You can change your life this moment. This very second you can say, "No more." Take a long, hard look at what's taking up too much space in your life. Do one significant thing about it. Do something that is so powerfully symbolic to yourself that you prove that you're serious. Draw a line in the sand. There is something in your life that you need to let go of. Take a deep breath.

You already know what it is, don't you?

5

The Gold Standard

You can count on me. You can believe in me. If I say I'll do something, I'll do it. Put it in the bank. Bet the farm on it. It doesn't matter whether or not I'm in a good mood, have a headache, forgot to pick up my clothes from the cleaners, had a fight with my daughter, lost my keys, or didn't sleep last night. If I said I'll do it, then I'll do it.

What's more, I'll do it every time.

If you can say all of that, and back it up, that's more than showing off. That's delivering the goods. That's the gold standard. If you consistently do what you say you'll do over a long period of time, the world will beat a path to your door. Nothing demonstrates the essence of showing off, in the most positive sense of the phrase, than rock solid consistency. There's an old saying that goes, "Amateurs work until they get it right. Professionals work until they can't get it wrong."

Think of someone you know or work with who is completely dependable. This is the person who, when given an assignment, simply carries it out, correctly and on time, every time. Giving them a job to do is like pulling the trigger on the starter's gun. You point them at a task and it is completed. You give them the tough assignment and you can forget about it, knowing that it's taken care of. How much value does that person bring to the table? It's as good as it gets.

We love people who do what they say they will do. Consistency is the foundation of success and the great business builder. Consistency is the definition of integrity. If that's showing off, then count me as someone who aspires to show off for as long as I live.

6

Get in the Damn
Boat and Go

Stop talking about what you could do, should do, or might do. Do it. At some point, you have to shut up and either do the thing that you say you want to do or just let it go. Take the trip, make the move, pierce the belly button, buy the house, apply for the job, ask her to dance, get the tattoo, or decide that you're not going to do it and move on to something that you *will* do. Columbus didn't spend all his life standing around arguing whether or not the world was flat. He finally said, "Guys, let's get in the damn boat and go. We may go over the edge, but it beats sitting around here."

In the 1980s, I learned a lot about the power of taking action when working with army officers. Each summer for five years, I led a series of one-week seminars on management and leadership, each of which ended with a two-day class project. What impressed me about these officers was that after I gave them the instructions for a rather complicated and involved project, they simply turned to each other, wrote their action plan, and got to work. When I did the same exercise with civilian groups, there were usually so many questions about what to do and how to do it that I finally had to cut them off so there would be time to do the project.

Think of the value you bring to your work if you are the one who takes the assignment and goes into action, instead of being one of the ones who ask question after question after question. Just do the thing! Trust your judgment and get on with it. Believe me, your value to your company and to your own career will skyrocket if you adopt the strategy of taking action rather than hesitating, questioning, and doubting.

Being known as the person who gets things done is one of the ultimate career turbo-chargers. When I ask managers and executives to rate, on a scale of 1 to 10, the value of an employee who takes action and gets things done, they invariably say, "10."

As a customer, a colleague, or an employer, I want to work with the person who finds the solutions and creates the opportunities, not the person who specializes in telling me why it can't be done. Hey, even if you look at this from the perspective of what is purely in your own self-interest, being action oriented beats doing nothing every time.

Top performers in any field or endeavor all have a strong propensity for action. It is the one essential first step. Go. Start. Do it now. Whatever it is you want to do, once you stop *talking* about doing it and actually start doing it, you will be amazed at what happens. You will start to experience the magic of people coming out of the woodwork to help you succeed. You will be floored at how circumstances seem to line up in your favor.

You will be equally amazed if your idea turns out to be really goofy and is a complete and total flop because, with that failure, you get a batch of new information that sets you on the right course. When you pick a cat up by the tail, you learn a lot about cats. You get scratched up but you learn a tremendous amount about cats. So pick the cat up. See what happens. Don't be stupid, but be daring.

With a willingness to take action comes a willingness to fail. When you take action, you'll make mistakes. When you make mistakes, you fix them. Mistakes are seldom fatal. What is fatal is the failure to take action in a constantly moving world. Don't avoid mistakes. Just be sure you avoid making the same mistakes twice. Learn from the mistakes.

You simply cannot be successful unless you are willing to fail. Here's the deal. If you ask her to dance, she might say no, but at least you stand a chance. But if you never ask her to dance, it's certain that you'll never dance at all.

7

As Good as You're Going to Be

Tiger Woods has a coach. Let's just sit with that one for a minute. Tiger Woods has a coach. That fact alone should be enough to make the point that you should never, ever, ever be as good as you're going to be. Inside every top performer is a better performer waiting to get out. The true spirit of showing off, in the best sense, is relentless improvement.

I like to think in terms of relentless improvement because the word *relentless* infuses power and passion into the idea of getting better each day. I want my pursuit of improvement to be truly relentless. Not because I'm noble or good. Not even because it's in the interest of my company or career. I want to get better every day because it's where all the fun is.

One of my favorite clients is a company that holds to the following standard for every employee, from the receptionist to the CEO: "If you're as good as you're going to be, you can't work here." They enforce that standard on everyone including the current crop of top performance award winners. Think about the power of that idea. If you're as good as you're going to be, you can't work here. Wow. Now that's a fun place to work because they keep it juicy. I can't imagine being bored working there.

I'm sure some think of relentless improvement as a burden. Fine. Stay the same. See how much fun that is. Do your work today just like you did it yesterday and see how far it gets you. It surely won't get you more than you got yesterday. Here's the rule: if you don't like what you're getting, then change what you're doing. What part of that is hard to understand?

Continuous improvement gets more lip service than almost any idea out there. I can stand before an audience of people from 50 different companies and ask, "How many of you believe that constant improvement is necessary to succeed in your business?" Every hand will go up. There's no debate. There's no disagreement. No one ever says, "Well now, hold on. I think that we can do perfectly well in our business if we pretty much just keep doing it the way we've always done it." Never. It simply doesn't happen.

But if I ask, "So what did you specifically do today that made you better than you were yesterday?" the mood in the room shifts dramatically. There is much eye contact avoidance and a great deal of hemming and hawing. If I press the question, I get responses like "Well, we were pretty busy today. We didn't really have time for improvement because there was so much to do."

Yeah, well, you missed the most important thing you had to do—to get better. You're toast, my friend, and the end is near. You're well on your way to becoming history. You just don't know it yet. Somewhere, while you're filling out the forms just like you did yesterday, one of your competitors took an hour to think about the form and realized that it's outdated, didn't serve any useful purpose, and eliminated it.

There's a very good indicator of whether or not you're in need of some serious improvement in what you do. If you feel absolutely comfortable with the way you do your work, then you're probably coasting on past success and you're not really serious about it.

Relentless improvement means that you're going to feel a little bit nervous because you're always going to be living close to the edge. If you're not living close to the edge, you're taking up too much space. There has to be that tension of trying something new and unknown.

Top performers are like top companies in that they invest considerable time and money in training. One of my clients recently said, "If any of our top performers begins to skip the training, we know that's the beginning of the end. The ones that stay on top are addicted to learning." Sometimes I'll hear successful people say things like "Let me tell you something. I've been around this block a lot of times. I know how this business works." If you ever hear me say something like that, please just slap me silly. Shake some sense into me, then kick my butt into some class or seminar that will wise me up to the fact that I'm just a dinosaur who knew how it worked in the old days, meaning last week.

Being better tomorrow than you were today is where all the joy, jazz, and kick are. It's where the juice is. It's where the fun is. It's where success is.

8

We See Things as We Are

We don't see things as they are. We see things as we are. There is always another way of looking at whatever's going on. As my friend, award-winning *National Geographic* photographer and nationally known speaker, Dewitt Jones says, "There's more than one right answer." When you let go of believing that there's only one right answer, you open the door to opportunity, innovation, solutions, and sometimes even boundless joy.

Old joke: A guy goes into the doctor's office. He moves his arm back and forth and says, "Doc, it hurts when I do that." The doctor says, "So don't do that." If the way you look at your life doesn't work, then don't do that. If you want to change your world, change your mind.

Here's the deal about reality: it depends on how you look at it. Literally. Totally. Your life is how you look at it because the way that you look at it is all that you've got. You never make a decision based purely on information. You're not wired that way. You first interpret the information. You look at it in a certain way. You put everything that you see, feel, hear, taste, and experience through a filter. It's your own very particular filter. Dewitt Jones says that the key to great photography is in choosing the right lens. Your filter, your lens, is the way you look at the world. This is your reality. There is nothing else.

Do you think that this is motivational, power-of-positive-thinking nonsense? If so, you are operating under a delusion. What you may need to do is let go of your particular filter. There are those who will say, "This is bull. Life is what it is and your attitude can't change one thing about it." And to them I say, "You, my friend, are a sissy. You're a baby and a whiner, and you don't have the guts or the courage or the creativity to do anything other than lay down and let life walk all over you." In life, problems and setbacks are mandatory. Misery is optional.

It's cold and rainy today. Is that good or bad? Well, it all depends, doesn't it? It depends on how you look at it. I know people that automatically define a rainy day as a bad day. That cracks me up. If you live where it rains 100 days per year, then you've automatically written off 100 days as bad days. My question is "Why?" Why would you choose that?

Are you getting uncomfortable with this discussion about perception? Does this kind of talk seem too much like positive attitude gibberish for you to stand it much longer? Wise up, sissy. This is about choices. It's about being smart and tough and seeing options.

Almost 30 years ago, I learned a significant life lesson from a coworker named Wayne Bredberg. Wayne was a poster boy for positive thinking. Wayne listened to motivational tapes. He read motivational books. His office space was decorated with motivational sayings. I thought Wayne was ridiculous. I thought he was gullible and naive. I, however, was tough and smart. I was a realist. I had no time for rah-rah motivational cheerleading.

I'll never forget the day that I confronted Wayne about his positive attitude. I said, "Wayne, all this motivational junk that you fill your head with is completely worthless. You think that listening to motivational tapes that tell you to wear a big, fat, happy, stupid smile on your face will make your life better. Well, it won't, Wayne. It's a myth. It's a little children's fairy tale. It's a waste of time, and it won't work."

Wayne smiled and calmly said, "Maybe you're right, Joe. Maybe it is a waste of time. And maybe it won't work. But, on the other hand, I'm happy and you're miserable." I simply stared at him. I had no response. He had nailed me right between the eyes. The truth was that Wayne's life did work better than mine because Wayne was tough enough and smart enough to find opportunity, while I was the wimp that waited for the world to treat me better. I was the "realist." Yeah, right. The truth is that I was the loser.

Even though I'm not crazy about the sometimes cheesy, over-the-top delivery of what is generally considered to be motivational thinking, I can't argue with one simple fact. If I can learn to change the way I look at my world, then I can change my world. If I can see opportunity where my competitor can't, then I win. If I can find solutions instead of only offering excuses, then I bring more value to the game.

I had a conversation with my friend Peter, whose job is to do the sound for movies. Peter told me that he had spent the summer working on a movie that was being shot in the Canadian Rockies. He said that he had to wear a heavy jacket every day throughout the summer and that he loved it. Imagine that. Cold all summer long. To him, it's heaven. To you, the ideal summer might be days of hot, sweaty, humid, jungle weather. Cool. Different strokes for different folks. The lesson for me is that it's not the weather that makes it a good day or not. It's never the weather. It's me. What I've got to do is either learn to use the weather I've got or get the heck out of Dodge to find the weather that I want.

Years ago when the Winter Olympics were being held in Canada, I remember that, during the men's downhill skiing event, all of the skiers were talking about how bad the snow conditions were. The temperature was warmer than anyone wanted and so the snow was a little mushy. I'll never forget how one contestant changed the conversation. In a television interview at the end of his first run, he said, "Everyone's making the mistake of thinking that it's about the snow. It's not the snow. It's never the snow. It's about how I ski the snow no matter what the conditions are." By letting go of the snow, this skier was opening the space to let his own strategy and ability become the most important factors.

Just recently, I faced a very similar "it's not the snow" situation. Much of my time is spent giving speeches at corporate conventions. There was an upcoming speech that I initially saw not only as being incredibly challenging, but also as potential trouble. Without going into detail, I'll just say that my particular speech assignment was extremely difficult. I spent a good part of one morning focused on the less than ideal circumstances I was facing.

Finally, something inside me said, "Joe, the way you're looking at this isn't working. Let it go." So I did. I let go of seeing this upcoming speech through the filter of a being a potential disaster and chose the filter of it being a potential victory. The key to this was not the circumstances but my ability to master the challenge and to figure out how to make myself the hero in the process. It's not the snow. It's never the snow.

If you want one power mantra for your work and your life, try this one: "There is another way of looking at this." I have a friend who believes that everyone is out to get him. Paranoia is his reality. Like most paranoid people, there's one big weakness in his thinking. He's really not that big a deal. People have way more important things to do than to spend their time plotting against him.

I choose to see the world very differently than he does. I suffer from reverse paranoia. I think everybody's out to help me. And guess what. They are. I make it up that they are, and they generally seem to go along with it. I approach people with the full expectation that they'll be on my side and damned if they aren't. Do you think that's naive of me? Well, I tend to get what I want. Do you?

All of this requires a certain degree of perspective. There are certainly circumstances in life that justify something more than just a shift in perception. If someone or something, for example, threatens the safety of my family, then I'm not going to work on letting go of the way I look at it. I will take action. I will do whatever is necessary to remove the threat.

Just because I choose to look at the world through a positive lens, don't make the very serious mistake of thinking I'm a pushover. Quite the contrary. Do not mess with me. You will regret it if you do. It's not those that are tough enough to make something out of difficult circumstances that are the pushovers. It's the bullies and the whiners who constantly complain that the world isn't fair. They'll crack like an egg when push comes to shove.

Very few situations will get absolute agreement from everyone on what the appropriate response or strategy should be, because we all look at things differently. The critical question here is that if something isn't working, how should I rethink it? It very likely may be the way you're looking at it that's got you stuck. Whatever the situation or problem is, always remember that there is another way of looking at it. Always. Whenever you think you've considered every perspective and possibility, remember that you haven't. There is one more.

What you want to do is create as many options as possible. Give yourself the widest range of choices in any situation. People usually have their own well-established personal pattern of reactions that limit their options. Some people have decided in advance that if they have a problem with a customer at work, it's a bad day. Other people have decided in advance that if they have a problem with a customer, it's a perfectly fine day with a perfectly normal problem to solve and it's the reason that they have a job.

What happens in the world is, quite literally, meaningless until you assign some meaning to it. Your view of the world is the only reality you have. Attitude, motivation, strategy, perception, style, personality, temperament, mood—they are literally our reality. Attitude is how you look at the world. If your attitude doesn't work, let it go and get another one.

If this all still sounds like some sort of motivational cheerleading session to you, then you miss the point. What some people call positive attitude is really about toughness, creativity, and courage. I know that this is a difficult concept for some people to deal with. I know because I used to be one of them. I found myself in a job surrounded by people who were consumed with positive thinking. It drove me crazy. I rejected the concept that I had control over my life through the choices I made. I hated knowing that I could just let go of the lousy way I looked at the world.

Why wouldn't I want to let go of not being in control? It's almost like a trick question. You can take control over your life and get what you want, but there's a catch. You have to let go of whining and making yourself miserable. Boy. Tough choice.

It really was a tough choice. If my one way of looking at the world is that I have no control, then that's my "Get Out of Jail Free" card, isn't it? I have a built-in excuse all ready to whip out whenever things don't go my way. If I let go of that, then I'm responsible. I'm in control. Oh my. I'm not sure I want to be in control.

I understand. I've been there. I've done that. But once I finally let go of being a victim of circumstances, my life changed forever. Everything shifted. I now fail on a regular basis, because I try a lot of new things. Some of them work. A lot of them don't. The difference is that I'm perfectly okay with that now, because I let go of the way I was looking at the world. I am now in charge. Things happen that I don't like, and I choose my response. This sets up the next thing.

It's not the snow. It's never the snow.

9

Stupid Promises

What would possess anyone in her right mind to promise more than she can deliver? Has she not experienced the frustration, disgust, and anger that come from being on the receiving end of broken promises? Does she honestly not realize the incredible damage that over-promising does in business and relationships? Show-offs never, ever promise more than they can deliver. Broken promises are stupid promises.

On a business trip to San Antonio, Texas, I checked into a hotel with signs everywhere proclaiming the hotel's new advertising campaign: *"Better* Than Our Competition." There was a big sign in the lobby, a little sign on the registration desk, a button on the desk clerk's lapel, another sign in the elevator, and little stand-up signs all over my room all of which said, *"Better* Than Our Competition."

Imagine my surprise and joy when I also discovered in my room that I had been named "Guest of the Month," which I gather was randomly selected. As "Guest of the Month," I got an ice bucket with a few longneck beers, a party tray with salsa and chips, and a straw cowboy hat. Cool. There was also a letter congratulating me on my good fortune on being selected, and asking me to perform a simple, yet important favor for the hotel.

In return for the goodies, I was asked to complete a fairly extensive feedback survey. They claimed to be *"Better* Than Our Competition" in all ways, and wanted to know how I thought they were doing. Fine. I popped open the first longneck and had at it. Boy, did they pick the wrong guy. Actually, they picked the right guy, depending on whether or not they used the information I gave them.

The feedback I gave them took the form of a major roasting. I hammered them, because I wanted to get their attention and have them realize the incredible folly of this absurd *"Better* Than Our Competition" marketing campaign of theirs. It's like some advertising android said, "Well, we know we're really not better than our competition, but to get better would take too much time and effort and money. So let's not really get better. Let's just say we're better, which will get us more customers and won't cost anything beyond a bunch of signs and lapel buttons!" Oh, yeah. That's marketing genius at work.

I'll not bore you with the list of deficiencies in that hotel, but suffice it to say that from the surly front desk clerk, to the somewhat dirty room, to the burned-out light bulbs, well, you get the idea. This hotel was far from even being up to par with their competition, much less being better than their competition.

If they hadn't brought it up, it wouldn't have been nearly as noticeable how truly deficient they were. I would have just chalked it up to another night in another thoroughly mediocre hotel. "*Better* Than Our Competition!" The nerve of such an obviously bogus claim made my head spin. As I drank more of the free beers, I had to get extra paper for my commentary, which was now approaching novella length.

Somewhere some knuckleheaded marketing guy or gal was proud as punch for coming up with such a clever and strikingly original (yawn) concept: "*Better* Than Our Competition." There's an old saying: "Don't wrestle with a pig. You just get all dirty and it annoys the pig." Let me add: "Don't claim to be something that you are not. You just look all stupid and it annoys everyone you come in contact with."

The very practical lesson for you and me in this tale of woe is about managing expectations. Don't make promises you can't keep. False promises not only work to destroy brands, they are among the deadliest career-busters of all time. Be accurate with your estimates of what you can do and when you can get it done. Never overpromise. From a major contract proposal to telling someone what time you'll be there for lunch, be realistic and deliver what you promise.

Great companies and top performers are masters at managing expectations and promising only what they can deliver. One of the tried-and-true examples of a great company is Southwest Airlines. Southwest has been talked about to death, but there's no denying this company's staying power as a first class show-off. What I find particularly fascinating about Southwest is that on their flights there's no food to speak of, no music, no videos to watch, and they have what some people refer to as a cattle call boarding process, although they are testing whether or not to change that.

But the key is that everyone knows the deal going in, and Southwest Airlines is perennially among the leaders in fewest customer complaints. They do what they say they will do. They do not promise you something and then fail to deliver on that promise. I constantly speak about how well Southwest Airlines manages their customers' expectations.

Do what you'll say you'll do. Don't promise what you can't do. False promises are stupid promises that will kill your career or your business.

10

Let's Be Too Much

Last year in a living room in Nashville, Tennessee, a woman named Rebecca Folsom sang a song that changed my life forever.

Did you ever hear a song that changed your life? I'm not talking about a song that you find really inspiring or that brings you to tears when you hear it. I'm not talking about a song that causes you to smile and dance for joy when it comes on the radio. I'm talking about a song that caused you to live your life differently. That's what happened to me.

My wife and I got an invitation to attend a house concert featuring Tom Kimmel, a longtime friend who is an amazing singer and songwriter. The opening act was a woman who I didn't know and had never heard before, Rebecca Folsom. It was just her and a guitar, and she was delightful. Her final song was called "Let's Be Too Much."

Ancient wisdom says that when the student is ready, the teacher will appear. I was ready. Rebecca Folsom appeared. She taught me with her song. As I listened to the words, it became more than entertainment. It was a lesson meant for me. I was at the right place at the right time of my life to hear the message of this song. I didn't realize how much it had affected me until days later, when it became clear that this song was not going to leave my head or my heart.

A song, a book, a poem, a painting, or any other expression of thought or feeling can affect someone profoundly if the time is right. The message of "Let's Be Too Much" may mean nothing to you, but it meant everything to me. Here are some of the lyrics:

> I've closed my doors, not to keep the world from
>   wandering in,
> But to keep myself in check, and the ripple I might
>   send.
> Is my smile too wide, my laugh too loud, my song
>   getting in?
> Spilling over me and over you—what a lovely mess
>   we're in.
> Let's be too much for this place
> Let's burn it down in a holy blaze
> Light our passion, scale the walls, over the edge like
>   it's nothing at all
> Free fall, free fall

Throw open your mind and let the dance begin.
Throw open your mind—release yourself to be
    carried on some wild wind.

As I said, these words might not mean much to you, but for me, they hit the proverbial nail on the head. More accurately, they lit my fuse. I had the realization as I listened to the song that Rebecca had expressed exactly what I wanted in my life. I had been feeling for quite some time that I was living in a rut, and I wanted out. It didn't mean that I wanted to run away from my life as it was. Indeed, what I wanted was to start to embrace my life. I wanted to feel fully engaged and stop playing everything so safe. I wanted, as the saying goes, to go for it. I wanted to "be too much."

Think about the words to this song. Have you closed your doors, not to keep anyone out, but to keep yourself in? Have you put a lid and a limit on who you are and what you can do with your life? Are you afraid that your smile, your laugh, and your song might be too much if you let it all loose?

When Rebecca sings, "let's burn it down in a holy blaze," it's not about destruction. It's about clearing the space for a new life to rise from the ashes. It's about hope and energy. The ideas of lighting my passion, scaling the walls, and letting the dance begin all spoke to me in such a way that I felt I had to either change my life and my work or I would explode with frustration. This song made me realize that I was playing it safe, thinking too small, and taking the path of least resistance.

I was doing work that was easy for me. Too easy. I wasn't being challenged creatively and that, for me, was akin to dying a slow death. I wasn't taking enough chances and the price for that was boredom. All my life I'd said that I'd rather be scared than bored, but I was violating that rule everyday. I was bored silly.

Inspired by "Let's Be Too Much," I began changing the nature of my work, specifically in the live presentations that I do for audiences. I produced a series of videos, including a music video of Rebecca performing "Let's Be Too Much." The videos added life and energy to my work. For the first time in years, I began to feel a sense of excitement and purpose about my work. Rebecca's song flipped an "on" switch in me that had been off for far too long.

There comes a time for most of us when we have to decide whether to give up, or to go for it. If you are at that point in your life, let me offer the best wisdom I know. Sometimes you have to say, "What the hell, I'm in."

Let's be too much. I'm in. How about you?

11

Imagination Will Take You Everywhere

The earth revolves around the sun. Everybody knows that. When it was first suggested by Copernicus and Galileo, however, they were thought to be madmen. Copernicus and Galileo did not create anything new. They simply looked at the same thing as everyone else and saw something different. They proposed a different context for understanding information that had been around forever.

Like all truly innovative ideas, the notion that the earth revolves around the sun, rather than the other way around, sparked notorious debate and fierce resistance. That's what happens when you throw a truly innovative idea onto the table. The exact same thing happens in corporate conference rooms around the world and in our own minds as we talk to ourselves. A new idea is considered crazy until it becomes what everyone knows.

Like the earth revolving around the sun, the next great idea for your business or career is most likely right in front of you in plain sight. You don't have to think it up. You don't have to be a wildly creative person to discover it. You just have to see it. Marcel Proust said, "The real voyage of discovery consists not in seeing new landscapes, but in having new eyes."

There's a great demand for consultants to come into companies and think up new ideas. That demand exists for the very same reason that there are fish markets. We'd rather pay someone to catch the fish than do it ourselves. But coming up with new ideas isn't really something that we need to pay someone else to do for us. It's simply a matter of learning to see, as Proust suggests, with new eyes. Innovation comes from practice and the discipline of always having your mental antennae out for a new way to look at existing information.

When you see the milk cartons being replenished at the supermarket, what do you see? Someone saw just-in-time delivery for the automotive market. That's where almost all innovative ideas come from. It's not the creation of something brand new, but instead the application of an idea from one arena to another. It's adaptive innovation. You can do this. Anyone can do this. It just takes practice.

In my book *Becoming a Category of One,* I wrote about Les Schwab Tires and their practice of someone running out to greet each car that pulls into their parking lot. It is a simple gesture that makes a big impression on customers. It's become their trademark. It sends a message that says, "You are the most important thing in our world."

So what's your version of running to the car? For me, it can mean taking the time to truly understand the nature of a client's business to the extent that no one else has. Or it can be one extra phone call to reassure her that everything is in place for the project. It might even be offering to write an article for a client's trade association magazine. I'm running to the car. How do you run to the car?

Consistently successful people look for ideas everywhere. They are idea sponges out to soak up inspiration from any source, anytime, anywhere. If they check in to a hotel and the process goes particularly well, they think, "That was easy. How easy are we to do business with? What are we doing that might potentially put up a barrier to doing business with us? How do we answer the phones? How easy is our web site to navigate? Are our invoices clear and easy to understand? What can we do that will make us be like this hotel's check-in process?" You don't have to come up with completely new ideas to innovate. You simply learn to use an existing idea in a different context.

If you have young children, you have built-in innovation tutors. When my daughter, Jess, was three years old, we did a project from one of her kid's magazines. We cut out little figures that, when folded in a particular way, were supposed to act like helicopters when you dropped them. They were designed to twirl delightfully down to a soft landing on the floor.

Our helicopters behaved more like rocks. Jess and I cut the figures out, folded them as instructed, and took turns dropping them. They fell straight to the floor with not a single twirl among them. After repeated attempts, and much frustration on my part, Jess suddenly shouted, "Wait, Dad! They're not helicopters. They're little people wearing vests. Look, they're a family. This one is the Dad and this one's the Mom and this one's the little baby."

The figures worked perfectly as little people. Jess was having a ball playing with this little helicopter family while I was having no fun at all, stuck in my idea of what the magazine had said they were supposed to be. I was limited by years of following instructions and coloring inside the lines. Jess, however, was unencumbered by any preconceived notion of what somebody else thought. Jess was an original. She was a critical thinker as only a three year old can be. I had logic on my side. Jess had imagination. It's not a fair fight. Albert Einstein said, "Logic will get you from A to B. Imagination will take you everywhere."

Sometimes the best ideas aren't logical at all; in fact, they're often counterintuitive. I read a report about a village in The Netherlands that had struggled for years with serious and sometimes dangerous traffic problems at their main intersection. They had used every kind of traffic sign and signal they could think of to solve the problem. Finally, they brought in a traffic flow consultant from London who studied the situation for a few weeks. When he submitted his proposed solution, the village leaders were stunned.

What the consultant proposed was that they take down all signs and signals and let the traffic go where it wanted to go. Let the traffic regulate itself. And, of course, it worked. The problem was solved with a completely counterintuitive solution. To regulate the traffic, don't put more rules on. Take all of the rules off. That's an interesting story, but what possible application could it have to you?

Possibly none for you, but the story made me start thinking about anything in my business where I faced a "traffic flow" problem. I began to consider how I charged certain consulting clients by the hour, and that it seemed that there simply weren't enough hours in my working days to go around. So I took down all the traffic signs and signals. I made myself available to my consulting clients on a 24/7 basis. They have unlimited access to me and can call at any time.

Take a wild guess. When my clients were given a limit on the hours they could call, the tendency was to use every last minute of every single hour so that they got the greatest value for their investment. When we changed the flow to unlimited access, it put the focus on what we were trying to accomplish, rather than the hours involved. They self-regulated and my time with them actually went down, while our productivity and their satisfaction went up.

If you're ever in Los Angeles International Airport, keep your eyes open for the free shoeshine stands. Yep. Free. The guy who owns these stands doesn't charge a penny. He, or one of his employees, will shine your shoes, be just as pleasant as pie, and simply turn to the next customer when finished. So how does he make money? Look at the tips that the people give him. I saw mostly $20 bills. People are so delighted by the service, the quality of the work, and the whole outrageous concept of the deal that they give him more than he would have charged them in the first place. That is so cool. It makes my head absolutely spin with ideas. If something like this doesn't make you think, I suggest you take your pulse. You might be dead.

It's a very powerful thing to make questions like "What if?" "Why not?" and "If not now, when?" or "If not us, who?" part of your regular conversations. The reason we're not more innovative is that the majority always shoots down innovation. Always. Remember, innovation can mean that, in adapting a new idea to your particular industry or field of endeavor, you're going first—which is a gutsy thing to do. Top-performing companies and individuals are those willing to make courageous decisions.

You have to constantly challenge assumptions and complacency. Your past success is probably the greatest enemy of your future success, because it can suck you into the black hole of thinking you know what works. At best, success means you know what used to work. Tomorrow's reality will require new solutions and will create new opportunities. If you're stuck in the way you always did it, you're doomed. Success is sometimes a lousy teacher. It can make you stop thinking.

The hard truth is that what you did to make you successful up to this point may be the very thing that's keeping you from going to the next level. In my business, the road to success is littered with the broken careers of people who were once masters of their craft, but they stopped learning and growing. Things were great, everybody was happy, and the money was rolling in, so why change? Because tomorrow the customer will want something better and different. You will either keep up or get left behind. There are lots of people who used to be top performers and who are now wondering what happened. They can succeed only in markets that no longer exist.

To me, business consists of pretty much two things: ideas and execution. My job is to come up with great ideas that enable me to create value for my customers. I then must execute those ideas in a way that works. It's been said that vision without execution is a hallucination. Execution is critical. I also must accept that the best execution of a bad idea won't work, either. But bad ideas come with the territory if you are an innovative thinker.

Perhaps my favorite bit of innovation wisdom comes from Thomas Edison, who said, "When you have exhausted all possibilities, remember this: you haven't." To me, the message is simply to keep thinking. Keep trying. Make mistakes; learn from them; and then apply what you've learned to the next idea. Mistakes won't kill me. Complacency will.

12

Get Back inside the Box

We can get so carried away with new ideas and thinking "outside the box" that sometimes we miss the greatest potential opportunity for significant improvement. With all of their innovative thinking, top performers are also constantly looking at the most basic elements of their business for opportunities to improve. It may be that while you're creatively brainstorming for exciting new ideas, you're losing customers because you're not meeting their basic expectations.

Sometimes you need to get back inside the box. What's the potential return if you significantly improve your delivery of core customer wants and needs? What if you come up with a better way of solving customers' everyday problems, instead of just coming up with something new? What if you focused on consistency of performance and absolute reliability, instead of adding a new buzzer or bell to your product?

You might be knocking yourself out to come up with a new menu item for your particular hamburger stand when what your customers really want is for you to just make sure the hamburger you're already selling is hot when they get it. What are you already doing that you can be better at? That might be the best investment of your time and efforts. Retool and upgrade what you're already doing and you may be surprised at the return on that investment. You have to be both a tortoise and a hare. You have to innovate while continuing to improve on core competencies.

What's your weakness? What is it that you're not so hot at? Your customers will tell you if you make them. Believe me, you'll probably have to make them. Most customers take the path of least resistance, which is to simply say nothing when they're not happy. You have to get them to tell you what you can do better. It's hard to hear it, but top performers are always hungry to know what they need to improve.

An oil company wanted to increase retail sales at the gas stations. The vice president in charge of the project said that her colleagues all wanted to come up with new offerings or services for customers, but she decided to ask the customers what was important to them before undertaking any action. A comprehensive customer survey revealed that what customers wanted at the gas stations were the basics, including gas pumps that work, shelter from the weather, to pay and exit quickly, reasonable cost, and clean restrooms.

The company committed to retrofitting. They redoubled their efforts to deliver on basic customer expectations. The result was a dramatic increase in sales and a double-digit return on capital. Great companies are always asking their customers what they truly value, then working to deliver on that expectation.

Customer feedback may indicate that your particular strength is in the sales process and initial delivery, but that you're lousy at follow-up and ongoing customer communications. Go to work. Get good at follow-up. Become a master of customer communications. It may be what you least enjoy doing but you don't build success just doing what comes easy to you. Buckle down and do the work you don't want to do, especially if that work is what you're weak in. It gets progressively easier and you get better the more you do it.

Interestingly enough, the most common mistake that I see people make is failing to improve what they're already good at. They usually want to come up with something entirely new to add to their bag of tricks, rather than focus on what they do really well but at which they could be truly amazing if they'd only kick it up a notch. The trap is an old nemesis—past success. If I know I'm good at something that has worked in the past, the temptation is to settle for my present level of performance.

When a star baseball player's strength is hitting, it doesn't mean that he stops working on it. If he hits 40 home runs in a season, then his quest should be to hit 50 home runs next season. If this same player's weakness is fielding, of course he'll work with coaches to improve that. The point is to be improving on all fronts all the time. But never become so enthralled by the siren song of doing something completely new that you forget to climb back inside the box and work on what you're already doing.

If you're not particularly good at some aspect of your work, get good at it. If you're great at something, get better at it. That's what showing off is all about. You never stop. You never get bored and the fun never ends.

13

Expect to Connect

Your willingness to connect with people is one of the most important success and happiness factors in your life. If you want to connect, you will. If you don't, you won't. It pretty much boils down to two rules. If you like people, they'll like you back. If you don't like people, they won't like you back.

My friend Jearlyn Steele is one of the most amazing singers I've ever seen perform. Jearlyn can absolutely knock the socks off everyone in her audience, and I've often wondered about the secret to her success. It goes beyond just great singing. It has something to do with her ability to make her performance connect with each person in the audience. When I asked Jearlyn about it, she simply said, "I expect to connect. I truly expect to connect."

If you're taking notes or highlighting anything in this book, highlight Jearlyn's statement: "I expect to connect." This is huge. This is the mother lode. This is the jackpot. If you approach your work and your life with the intention of "I expect to connect," there is no possible way that you will not succeed. It's the essence of showing off in the best way.

Think about every person in the past three days that has made a favorable impression on you. What was the common factor in every single one of those interactions? A connection was made. It might have lasted no more than a few seconds, but a connection was made.

Jearlyn says that connecting is a matter of making "the love get bigger." She said, "There are people that will hear this and they'll say, 'Ha. It's not about love, Jearlyn; it's not about love.' But it is so about love." Jearlyn and I are in complete agreement that, at the end of the day, it's all a love thing.

Do you want your customers to love doing business with you? Of course you do. I have never had anyone tell me otherwise. But do you talk about love at work? Probably not. Well, why not? How can you want people to love doing business with you and not talk about love? It makes no sense. Is it because we lived in such a completely screwed-up world that it's become inappropriate to talk about love? Don't tell Southwest Airlines (stock symbol: LUV). They talk about love all the time. It's part of their strategy. Why would it not be?

Everybody wants love. It's the most basic human need. The great shame and waste is that we usually find it so uncomfortable to talk about love. But whether you call it love, engagement, connecting, or something else, the fact is that it's what makes the world go around. This isn't something that needs explaining, even in a business context. Everybody "gets it"; to succeed in business or in your career, you have to connect. The problem is that we don't pay enough attention to it. We're not intentional about it.

Jearlyn absolutely nailed it when she said that she goes to work with the thought: "I expect to connect." Wow. Think about the power of that idea. If you went to work everyday with the intention of making a connecting with every person you came in contact with, what a profound difference it would make.

Connection can be something as simple as making eye contact. It can shift your entire world. Try it for one day. For 24 hours, simply make real eye contact with everyone you interact with. It doesn't have to be forced and it certainly shouldn't be something uncomfortable. I'm not talking about staring people down. Just look that customer or coworker in the eye long enough to make a connection. When the person in the coffee shop hands you your order, make eye contact long enough to acknowledge her. It's magic. It will completely change your mood and how you feel about yourself and the world.

Making meaningful connections is about doing small things with attention and intention. Attention means focusing on both the person and the task, working with care, and caring about the person who you're doing it for.

Intention means being there — really being there and not just going through the motions.

To me, working with attention and intention is the very best of showing off. It's easy to think that showing off means doing something outrageous or over the top, but that's usually not the case at all. To me, the best show-offs are people who are so smooth and understated at what they do that you hardly notice them, but you definitely notice the magic they create. Showing off is not about doing big things or being a superstar. Showing off is about small things done with attention and intention.

Is our intention to just sell stuff, or are we there to help people? There's a difference. Do you have the intention of just getting through the day, or of making the day count for something? There's a big difference.

It's also a matter of attention, and of knowing that the seemingly small things count for a great deal in connecting with people. I was recently hired to help a hospital with their "Focus on Our Customer" campaign. I remember that a doctor raised the question of how patients can believe that the hospital truly cares when it's next to impossible for anyone to find a parking space there. It's so easy to think that our core product or service is all that really matters when, in fact, it's the total experience that we create that ultimately makes a connection or leaves people cold. If you make it a challenge to get into your parking lot, then please don't tell me how much you care about me.

Connecting with people through small things done with attention and intention can be achieved by any person and any organization, but it won't happen because of a memo, motivational signs in the employee cafeteria, or the occasional mention at staff meetings. Connection happens when you think about it, talk about it, and model it all day long, every day. It's what top performers focus on all the time.

At the end of the day, making connections with people is a matter of truly engaging with them. It's a matter of being there with intention and not "mailing it in" or just going through the motions. And, as Jearlyn said, when you connect, it's you who benefits. When you make a connection, you feed your own spirit.

I was in a hotel in Columbia, South Carolina, years ago, and as I walked down the hallway I passed by one of the housekeeping staff. She flashed me the warmest, most wonderful smile I'd ever seen. I said, "You know, that smile makes me feel better." She looked me right in the eye and said, "You know, it makes me feel better, too." It was a 10-second encounter, but the connection she made with me was powerful enough to stay with me all these years.

Expect to connect. It's a code to live by.

14

Going All In

There's a cultural phenomenon that's been sweeping the land: poker as a spectator sport. My gosh, is this a great country, or what? Poker is America's newest spectator sport. It gives new meaning to the term *couch potato*. We can now sit in the comfort of our living rooms and watch, with no physical exertion on our own, men and women sit around a table and play cards.

Let me be the first to admit that I find myself occasionally hooked by the high drama of watching people playing poker for big money. Poker has everything—deception, intrigue, fear, and a generous dose of showing off. There is usually a wide range of personality types around that final table where some winner will take it all. There's the obnoxious, loudmouth braggart that you love to hate. There's the mysterious young dude in sunglasses who doesn't let on that he's even breathing. There's the woman who played her way through the male-dominated poker world to take her rightful place with the masters. Then there's the old guy in the cowboy hat that is beloved by all, including his competitors. It's pretty much everything you need for a great night's entertainment on the big screen television.

Recently, Reverend Jim Kitchens, the minister of our church and a self-confessed poker fan, gave a sermon on the concept of "going all in"—the moment of truth for a poker player. "Going all in" is when that player bets every last chip on one hand. She'll either win the pot and live to play another hand, possibly win everything and be the champion, or lose it all and go home empty-handed. It's an electric moment and it's what poker players and fans live for—the feeling of everything being on the line with nothing held back.

Jim used "going all in" as a metaphor for depth of commitment. It was one of those sermons that made you squirm in your seat because it forced you to take an honest look at your life and what you claim is truly important to you. You had to see if what you say matches up with how you live.

I think it's useful to do an inventory of whether or not I've gone all in with what I say I value. In my work, am I all in when it comes to being of service to my customers? How about my loyalty to my coworkers or colleagues? Am I all in when it comes to following my own dreams and goals? Have I put every chip in the pot in terms of my family? My faith? My community? My friends? Am I all in?

I've spent almost three decades working with companies and individuals on how to improve performance. If I could give you just one idea on creating optimum personal performance, it would be this: Go all in. Whatever your skill level, expertise, advantages or disadvantages, if you or your team are truly all in, then there is no way that I would bet against you. I've seen it over and over in countless examples of a seemingly unlikely person or team not only achieve their stated goal, but exceed it. The most important factor in their success was that they were completely and totally committed with all of their hearts.

Look at your own experience. You may be just getting by in your work, but you are the star of the weekend softball team. What's the difference? I would wager almost anything that you're all in on the softball but halfhearted about the work. If that's the case, then what's the answer? How can you be as good at the work as you are at the softball?

You either go all in with the work you've got or find some other work that you can go all in with. If your choice is to find other work, then get busy. Take the steps that will lead you to a more fulfilling job. If you feel like you should stay where you are, then get busy creating the "all in" mindset toward it. For a lot of people, this is a monster challenge. I understand it. I have experienced it. I sometimes still experience it.

One thing that has always irritated me is this idea that if you just "follow your passion," the windows of heaven will open up and shower you with success and peace of mind and life will be a bowl of self-actualized cherries. Right. If only it were that simple. My problem is that I'm not completely sure what my passion is when it comes to work. I like writing a lot. I enjoy giving speeches. But what I'm truly passionate about is my family and friends. Maybe I'm a slacker at heart. My passion lies in hanging out with people I like.

Rather than quit work and go on a sabbatical to discover some burning career passion, which, by the way, might be just the ticket for some people, I've decided to go all in with my work because, well, it's my work. Seriously. I decided that whatever work I do can be a source of fulfillment and even joy, depending on the extent to which I go all in with it.

It can be a chicken-or-egg question. Should I wait until I find work that I love before I commit to go all in? Or should I go all in so that I will begin to love the work that I've got?

It's like the street sweeper who decides to be the best street sweeper in the history of the world because it just doesn't make any sense to approach it any other way. Why would I conceivably not want to be the best I can be at whatever I'm doing? I like the idea that whether I'm sweeping a street, weeding my yard, playing drums in a band, teaching a class, taking photos at a wedding, working as a customer service representative, selling insurance, washing cars, running a company, being a personal fitness trainer, bagging groceries, or writing a book that I take the attitude that I will knock your socks off with how I do what I do. Or maybe it's my own socks that I want to knock off.

It's why people climb mountains. Because they're there. Why would I want to go all in with my work? Because it's there. That is all the reason that anyone needs. The bigger question is, why would you not go all in?

15

Joe and Muhammad

It's easy to find show-offs in sports, so let's go there. Let's see what we can learn about working like you're showing off from some amazing athletes. Let's visit my own personal Sports Show-Off Hall of Fame. You don't have to be a sports fan to get the lesson. You just have to be human.

When I was a kid growing up in the 1950s and 1960s, my sports heroes were the rebels who could deliver on their promises. While all the other guys I knew were fans of professional quarterback good guys Bart Starr and Johnny Unitas, I was a fan of Joe Namath. Bart Starr and Johnny Unitas were the classic heroes. They were the cowboys in the white hats. Joe Namath was much more of a bad boy. The establishment hated Joe Namath. He was brash and showy. He wore full-length fur coats and had a bar in New York called Broadway Joe's. And most people thought that he talked too much.

Before his New York Jets played the Baltimore Colts in Superbowl III, he did the unthinkable. He guaranteed a victory. The Jets were extreme underdogs. No one believed that they could beat the Colts. But Namath guaranteed it. You may be too young to remember how it was in professional sports back then, but take my word for it, you simply didn't do that sort of thing in that era.

The Jets beat the Colts. I was one very ecstatic 15-year-old boy.

A few years ago, I found myself sitting next to Joe Namath on a flight from Los Angeles, California, to Palm Springs, Florida. I didn't say anything beyond a simple hello to Namath until the end of the flight. As we stood in the aisle of the plane, waiting for the door to open, I said, "I'm a fan of yours, Joe. When you guys beat the Colts, it was one of the best days of my life." He smiled and said, "Thanks. It was one of the best days of my life, too."

Joe Namath happened to be a rather loud and highly visible show-off. But he backed up his words with action. He did what he said he was going to do. He's who they're talking about when they say, "It ain't bragging if you can do it."

During that same era, I was about the only kid I knew in Springfield, Tennessee, who was a fan of a heavyweight boxer named Cassius Clay, who later changed his name to Muhammad Ali. It seemed like everybody hated Ali except for me and sportscaster Howard Cosell. Most people I knew didn't like Cosell, either. They considered him and Ali both to be nothing more than obnoxious show-offs.

Ali was an audacious showman who loudly proclaimed himself to be "the greatest fighter of all time!" Ali set new standards when it came to showing off, and it wasn't hot air. A poll of boxing experts on ESPN sports television has named Muhammad Ali the greatest fighter, not just heavyweight, but in all weight classes, of all time. Ali not only revived the sport of boxing, he redefined it. Ali understood the principle of making an emotional connection with the fans. It might be a positive connection, or a negative one. You might see him as the hero, or as the villain. But either way you couldn't ignore him. He was a force of nature.

Recently, in the Cincinnati Airport, I saw a long line of people snaking through the terminal. All kinds of people—young and old, black and brown and white, male and female—were making their way toward something that stirred my curiosity and I had to discover what it was. I found a vantage point where I could see the object of their excitement. It was Muhammad Ali. By this time in his life, Ali had developed that tremor in his limbs and voice, and he was greeting his fans while sitting down.

But the spark was still in his eyes, and as they had their photos taken with him, he was more than willing to strike that trademark show-off pose of biting his lower lip and drawing back his fist as if to unleash a thundering blow. The people loved this man. You could see it in their eyes.

Decades earlier, most of the country considered him a blowhard show-off, but, partly because Ali consistently delivered on his promises and had the courage of his convictions, he has become a truly beloved figure, not only in the United States, but also throughout the world. Who could forget the Olympics in Atlanta when Muhammad Ali lit the Olympic flame to begin the games? It was as inspiring a moment as any of us have ever seen.

Joe Namath and Muhammad Ali fit the traditional mold of showing off in the sense that they seemed larger than life. To me, there was always something playful in their swagger and over-the-top outspoken ways. There was a gleam in their eyes that let me know that they were just having fun. There was nothing mean or malicious about them. They were like kids. They were celebrating the joy, jazz, and kick of being the best at what they did.

Equally if not even more impressive to me are the sports figures that do what they do quietly and without fanfare. Athletes like soccer star Mia Hamm, tennis players Chris Evert and Martina Navratilova, baseball legend Cal Ripken of the Baltimore Orioles, professional golfer Nancy Lopez, and football greats Steve Largent and Eddie George embody a style of showing off that is almost elegant in nature.

To be extraordinary at what you do and do it with understated class is, to me, the ultimate in showing off. If you watch a professional football game today, it seems that there's as much competition to come up with the most outrageous touchdown celebration as there is to score the touchdown itself. What I loved about Steve Largent and Eddie George was that when they scored, they acted like they had been there before. Their attitude seemed to be, "This is my job. This is what I do."

Whatever the particular style of showing off, the bottom line is whether or not you do the job. For most of us, it's not about scoring touchdowns or shooting par. It's about making sure that the computer glitch is solved, the delivery is made on time, or the sale is completed. Whatever arena you play in, the joy is in making the play. The reward can be found, not just in the pay you receive for the work, but also in the work itself. That's your choice to make.

16

We Haven't Seen That

It can happen at work, a party, or a business conference. It can happen anywhere. For some people, it seems to happen almost all the time. You look around and think to yourself, "I'm a fake. I'm the only one here who doesn't have a clue what's going on. Everyone else is cool and in charge and totally on top of things. I'm completely lost. I'm a total fraud and I'm going to get busted."

Okay. So let's assume that you don't know what you're doing. Well, don't sweat it too much because neither does anybody else. Just read the newspaper and you'll see. Tell me who knows what they're doing. Economists? Ha. Economists only exist to give astrologers credibility. Political leaders? They don't have any more of a clue than you or I. Business gurus? Most of them are just guessing.

Here's the scoop on not knowing what you're doing: None of us do. To one degree or another, we're all making it up as we go along. Don't let that stop you. Maya Angelou once said, "Each time I write a book, every time I face that yellow pad, the challenge is so great. I have written eleven books, but each time I think, uh oh, they're going to find me out. I've run a game on everybody and they're going to find me out." Here's a woman who is absolutely brilliant, successful, and totally respected, and she's got the same insecurities as you and me.

The trick is to figure out what you're all about and run with it. Forget about who you think you're *supposed* to be. Who *are* you? Stop trying to be some idealized version of somebody else. If you're trying to be Madonna or Donald Trump or Mother Teresa, give it up. It's already been done by the originals. And besides, we've already seen them.

Be you. We haven't seen that.

17

The Pursuit of Happiness

Let's consider the pursuit of happiness. This is a controversial subject that always gets people riled up. There's a considerable difference of opinion over the worth or appropriateness of happiness as a pursuit. Henry Drummond said, "Half the world is on the wrong scent in the pursuit of happiness. They think it consists in having and getting, and in being served by others. On the contrary, it consists in giving, and in serving others." However, Albert Einstein had this to say, "Well-being and happiness never appeared to me as an absolute aim. I am even inclined to compare such moral aims to the ambitions of a pig."

As you thoughtfully choose your goals and pursuits, I submit the Declaration of Independence for your consideration. The founding fathers were not a frivolous group.

When writing the Declaration of Independence, they took great care in choosing each word. Their intention was that their words be taken very seriously. The second section of the Declaration reads: "We hold these truths to be self-evident, that all men are created equal, that they are endowed by their Creator with certain unalienable Rights, that among these are Life, Liberty and the pursuit of Happiness." I suggest that you take "the pursuit of Happiness" very seriously. They did.

Here's the bottom line. The pursuit of happiness sets you on the path of highest productivity. That's not motivational cheerleading. That's about being smart, focused, and intentional in your work and your life. If you're doing work that doesn't make you happy, then you most likely won't be very good at it. If people working together don't make each other happy, then they probably aren't a very effective team. If you are not happy, then you stand very little chance of success.

I started my career in real estate sales. I was good at selling, but I didn't really enjoy it. What I discovered I was good at and also enjoyed was teaching selling skills to others. I loved teaching people how to do what I could do. This led to me becoming the sales manager, then general manager, and then moving to a much larger company where I was director of marketing. That path ultimately led me to becoming a writer and consultant on personal performance. Voila!

I pursued both what I was good at and what made me happy and it took me, and continues to take me, to my highest level of personal performance. I will say it over and over: "Don't get stuck doing something you're good at." If it doesn't make you happy, consider yourself warned. You're in for trouble down the road.

But what about the broader view on happiness? Is it the ultimate goal? Should it be the goal? Or was Einstein right? Are you the moral equivalent of a pig if you're trying to be happy?

Here's a conversation on the subject of happiness:

I don't like this question. "Are you willing to be happy?" I don't like what it implies.
Like what?

That being happy is a worthy goal. It just strikes me that having your life's goal to be happy is somewhat shallow.
Ah. Shallow. Not meaningful enough. Not deep enough.

Don't be condescending. It's not a matter of being deep. It's a matter of not being selfish. Life should be about caring, giving, and accomplishment.
Let me get this straight. To you, being happy means being selfish.

No, but setting happiness as your number one goal in life means being selfish.
Well, what makes you happy?

What makes me happy is being with and taking care of my family, and making a contribution to the lives of others.

Beautiful. So your goal is to do those things that make you happy.

But, and this is a big but, being happy is a by-product of what I do. It's not the goal. The goal is to help people.

I must admit, it sounds nobler that way.

You're being sarcastic. Does that make you happy?

Good point. Actually, being sarcastic, which I've done way too much in my life, makes me feel like a jerk. What makes me happier is recognizing when I am sarcastic, and working on not being so sarcastic. I apologize.

Apology accepted. But we digress.

No. On the contrary. This is the whole issue of happiness. There are things I do that bring me joy; a warm feeling; a sense of accomplishment, contentment, or victory over the forces of evil; or whatever. Regardless of the activity, like apologizing sincerely when I do something hurtful, the common factor among all of the good things that I do is that I am happier for having done them.

Then you think we only disagree over semantics?

Partially. I certainly allow that people are motivated by different things. I'm sure there are lots of people who find it more effective to focus on the act itself, whether it's helping people or eating an ice cream cone, rather than the resulting feeling.

But let's get back to the question of perspective. Isn't it inherently better to focus on the act of giving than to focus on the happiness that the act brings to the giver?

Inherently better? I honestly have no response to that. Better according to whom? Society? Your friends? Here's my point: happiness has gotten a bad rap. I remember times when people, maybe just for the sake of conversation, have posed the question "What is your goal in life?" or "What is the point of our existence?" The most popular answer, meaning the one I've heard given most often, is usually along the lines of "to make a difference," "to help others," or "to make the world a better place." It's much more acceptable to people to answer the "What is your goal?" question like a Miss America contestant. Say something noble. Then I chime in with "To be happy," and there is usually a somewhat stunned and embarrassed silence followed by someone saying something like "Well, I certainly think there's more to life than that," or "It seems to me that surely we're here to accomplish more than just have a good time."

Okay. You gave me something to think about. I don't think I agree with you, but I'll think about it.

A friend of mine, who asked for my response to the question "What is our purpose here on earth?" in preparation for a guest sermon he was going to give at his church, was clearly disappointed with my "To be happy" answer. I think he wanted something loftier. But consider what Joseph Fort Newton had to say about happiness: "To be happy is easy enough if we give ourselves, forgive others, and live with thanksgiving. No self-centered person, no ungrateful soul can ever be happy. Life is giving, not getting."

Some people immediately think that being happy must mean leading a life of self-indulgent, meaningless, somehow destructive activity. It is odd to me that anyone would reach that conclusion. Most of the people I've known who lead a life of self-indulgence and shallow, meaningless activity are, in fact, usually not happy at all. The philosopher Wu Wei Wu said, "Why aren't you happy? It's because ninety-nine percent of everything you do, and think, and say, is for yourself."

The happiest people I know are good, caring, wonderful people. The best people I know—the genuine show-offs among us, those who truly do make a contribution—are usually very happy. They want goodness in life not just for themselves, but for others. They give a lot. Good people. Fulfilled. Happy.

Wise up. Life generally works pretty well. A state of perpetual unhappiness is probably a sign that you are making some choices that are screwing up the natural order of things. A state of martyrdom, that is, the pain that comes from sacrifice and giving until it hurts, is baloney. If you feel sorry for yourself for giving so much, then you're giving with resentment and attachment. It taints the gift. The point isn't to give until it hurts. The point is to give until it feels good.

My experience is that truly giving people are generally truly happy people. And never think that having problems means you must be unhappy. Problems are part of the natural order of things. Of course, I'm not talking about people who are dealing with tragic circumstances. That's another subject. I'm talking about most of us who have to deal with the pain and struggle of living every day in an imperfect world.

Every happy person I know has bad days. There are days when they are depressed, down, or have the blues, all of which can and do happen within the context of a happy life. Within a happy life are times of grief, despair, anger—the whole range of human emotions. To me, a happy life means a complete life. All of it. The painful as well as the joyful.

Life finds its purpose and fulfillment in the expansion of happiness.

—Maharishi Mahesh Yogi

18

The Enemy of
Future Success

Maybe your life has worked pretty well to this point. You've made a go of it with your career and things are rolling along pretty well. But you want more. You want to take your job or your business or some other aspect of your life to the next level. But you just can't seem to get any upward momentum going.

Here's your obstacle: if you are successful, then you know what used to work. The key word is "used" to work. Past tense. Gone. Over and done with. Obsolete. Outdated. Useless. In the way.

Past success is possibly the most challenging obstacle to your ability to move your life to the next level. You have succeeded by doing things a certain way. Why should you possibly let go of what has worked for you up to now? Because past success can be, and usually is, the enemy of future success.

My business has been very successful. I am blessed beyond reason. And I'm good at what I do. But for me to take my business to the next level of success and accomplishment, I have to be willing to let go of what got me to this point. It's been said that success makes obsolete the very behaviors that created it. Success creates a new reality and with it comes a new set of rules and challenges.

I hate hearing that. I hate it because it means that I have to think about letting go of what I'm good at, comfortable with, and used to. It means that I have to change even though things aren't really all that bad just as they are. I hate it. So I start to tell myself how really great I am at what I do. I've conquered the markets that I compete in and why the heck should I change what works?

On days that I find myself feeling just a little too cocky, I always try to remember this simple truth: I can compete and win in markets that *no longer exist*. They're gone. They're over. Today is a new day with new rules and new realities, and I have to figure out how to win today, not yesterday.

Your greatest challenge isn't to learn something new, it's to unlearn a lot of what you already know. Dee Hock, the founder of Visa, said, "The problem is never how to get new, innovative thoughts into your mind, but how to get the old ones out." One of the best ways to clear out your mind is to spend as much time as possible with people who see the world very differently from you. If everyone you hang out with is just like you, your brain is just taking in the same ideas over and over. You need a new filter. Get some new friends with a different way of looking at life.

Don't think that I'm saying you should throw out everything you believe in. Most of us form a set of values we believe in that may serve us well for a lifetime. For me, those values include things like finding a way to create winners instead of losers, treating people with kindness and respect, playing for long-term success rather than immediate rewards, and endeavoring to always do the right thing. I don't necessarily succeed at following those values all of the time, but I know that they work.

Fundamental values don't take up space that I need for new ideas for future success. They are the foundation on which that success will be built. What takes up space are the ways of doing business and living my life that may still seem to work, but that are the very things that are keeping me from getting to the next level of performance.

What's that old saying? That insanity is doing the same thing over and over and yet expecting a different result. What's your particular insanity? What are you still doing that you know you have to let go of in order to move on? Even if you can identify it, it's hard to let it go, isn't it? That's because you're good at it. It's comfortable.

Bite the bullet. Look at everything that has worked for you up to this point, and then summon the courage necessary to let go of whatever part of it is holding you back. You know what it is. It's just a matter of doing it.

19

What You Think of Me Is None of My Business

I've spent way too much of my life trying to get other people to like me, approve of me, and accept me. It's ludicrous. It's a stupid waste of time. It's even worse than a waste of time; it's dangerously counterproductive. The truth is that other people are too busy thinking about themselves to pay that much attention to me one way or another. The truth is that if I spend my time trying to make everybody else happy, then I'll be emotionally empty and won't be any fun to hang out with anyway. The truth is that if I do everything to get you to like me, then I'll probably end up staring in the mirror and realizing that I don't even like myself because of the whimpering wimp that I've become.

What you think of me is none of my business. That doesn't mean that I should be rude or uncaring. Quite the contrary. I've found that the people in my life who are the kindest, the most generous, and the easiest to get along with are the ones who know who they are, are confident in themselves just as they are, and can meet the world with love and open arms because they're not playing mind games to win my approval. They've let go of my approval and given themselves their own stamp of approval.

Think about the people you know who are pleasures to be around. Are they the ones who are constantly talking about themselves and trying to impress you with their great accomplishments? Are they the ones who will change their opinions to suit whoever they happen to be with at the time? Are they the ones who say whatever they think you want to hear? No. Those people are generally irritating, if not a flat-out pain in the ass.

The people that are, in fact, a pleasure to be around are the ones who have let go of what you think of them. They are likeable because they like themselves. They aren't arrogant, but they are sure of themselves. They can give love to others because they have a healthy self-love. You respect them because you know where they stand. They are the people who have given up worrying about whether or not they're making you happy with everything they say or do. They focus on doing what makes them feel good about themselves. Not in a selfish way, but in a way that flows from values that count for much more than being popular.

It's one of the most counterintuitive ideas around, but it's true. The most loving people in the world don't care what you think about them. They just care about you. There's a difference.

20

Whatever Happens
Is Normal

Nothing is good or bad but that our thinking makes it so.
—William Shakespeare

What's the difference between the person who easily and gracefully handles the unexpected and the person who goes ballistic over the unexpected? It's the Normal Factor. The person who handles the unexpected has decided that whatever happens is normal—but not acceptable, necessarily. Sometimes things happen that are terrible. Sometimes these things are seriously terrible, like destructive tornadoes, life-threatening illnesses, or auto accidents. Sometimes they are just irritatingly terrible, like stepping on gum in a movie theatre. All are terrible to one degree or another—completely unacceptable—but normal in that they are simply a part of life as we know it.

We have to learn to accept life on its own terms. Things aren't the way they're supposed to be. They are the way they are. The way you deal with it makes the difference. If you accept that even bad things are normal, you are much better equipped and prepared to handle them, to minimize the damage, to correct the problem, or to even create opportunity from the problem! If you have a very narrow definition of what's normal, you are much more likely to throw up your hands in despair when things happen that don't "suit" you.

One of the best ways to observe the "whatever happens is normal" concept in action is to watch people when they travel. People tend to let their goofiness truly shine through when they face the everyday challenges of travel in today's world.

I was flying into Chicago, Illinois, in January. No snow had been predicted, but as we approached O'Hare Airport for our landing, there was snow. And plenty of it. Flying into the surprise blizzard, I listened to the comments of those sitting around me:

"Holy cow! Look at this snow! Whadda we do now??!"

"Good grief! It's snowing! This messes up everything!"

"Snow! I can't believe it! Snow! This is terrible!"

The cabin of the airplane was thick with exclamation points.

I was sitting there thinking, "I'm sorry. Is it just me? It's CHICAGO!!! It's JANUARY!!! DUH!!!" Snow in Chicago in January is normal. I struggle with the concept that people would let snow . . . in Chicago . . . in January . . . tear them to pieces.

Change gears. From Chicago to a vacation trip I took years ago. A Mediterranean cruise. Every evening a particular couple would complain about something. Anything. Everything. You could count on this couple (the Whiners, as we all came to know them) to find something in that day's activities that had made them unhappy.

The final day trip of the cruise was a delightful North African excursion. We were in Tunis, Tunisia, riding on a bus that was technically air-conditioned, but hot. Very hot. Everyone was very warm and very sweaty but having a fine time because we were driving through desert sand and passing guys on camels and it really felt kind of good and appropriate to sweat. It just seemed to fit, somehow. It was a good, sweaty situation.

That night, in the ship's meeting room, the Whiners told the cruise director how very unhappy they were and demanded a refund because the bus was too hot and that back home their house was air-conditioned and people shouldn't have to be uncomfortable from the heat, and so on. The cruise director took all he could stand and finally said, "Let me give you two a little travel tip. If you want things to be the way they are at home . . . STAY THE HELL AT HOME! IT'S AFRICA!!!" All of the other passengers started screaming, "Overboard!! Throw them overboard!!!" Africa is hot. Hot in Africa is normal. If you don't want hot, don't go to Africa.

Next time you're at an airport and flights get delayed or cancelled, don't miss the opportunity to watch and learn. You are in an incredible human laboratory for the observation of people and their reactions to the unexpected. Watch for the Victims. The Victims are the people who are convinced that the world is out to get them. That everyone has plotted against them and is dedicated to making them miserable. What kind of an inflated ego do you have to have to believe something like that?

What the Victims don't recognize is that it's not about them. I mean, get real. The airlines are not out to get them. But the Victim will cry and whine and moan, "Woe is me. My flight was cancelled and the world is a terrible place. How unfair. Boo hoo hoo."

Please. Flights get cancelled everyday. It is normal. It is inconvenient, frustrating, and even maddening, but it is also normal.

"Excuse me, I'm in an airport. Do flights ever get cancelled here?"

"Why, yes. As a matter of fact, they do!"

"Ah. Good. Then I'm on the right planet."

Then there's the Tough Guy (male or female). Tough Guys won't get pushed around. If there's a monsoon hurricane that causes their flight to be cancelled, they take action. They take names. They threaten to have people fired. They do all manner of utterly idiotic, ineffective, and irrational things to prove that they are mad as hell, and they won't take it anymore.

The problem is that Tough Guys try to bully their way through every situation that doesn't suit them. Most of the time, on this planet, bullying is a stupid and counterproductive way to go about getting what you want. It has the reverse effect. Bullying invites resistance.

So, you're stuck in an airport. You have to wait for hours. This happens. It is normal. And, having decided that it is normal, you don't go crazy. You consider your options. What would you do? What could you do? Hmm-mmm. Let's tap on our thinking tooth and see what we can come up with that will minimize the damage, make a lousy situation bearable, make a lousy situation pretty good, or actually create an opportunity.

You could phone home, walk around and get some exercise, zone out and get some sleep, shop and buy something fun, people-watch and enjoy the show, get something to eat, get a beer, make new friends, read a trashy novel, read something serious and get smarter, do your expense report, catch up on some work, write some emails, watch a DVD on your computer, listen to Rebecca Folsom on your iPod, or write a book (this one was partially written in airports, believe me)—the list goes on and on and on.

The point being that any of these options are better than being the Whiner or the Victim or the Tough Guy. This is not brain surgery. Well, maybe in a way, it is.

Make good choices. Why do some people, me included, find that so hard to understand?

> The mind is its own place,
> and in itself can make a heaven of hell,
> or a hell of heaven.
> —John Milton

21

Guess What I Want and Other Stupid Mind Games

Here's a fun game to play with a coworker. For even more fun, play it with your spouse or significant other. It's called "Guess What I Want." By the way, show-offs never play this game.

Guess what I want. I'm not going to tell you. That would be too easy. You have to guess. If you don't give me what I want, I will resent you and play another game with you. It's a game called "Nothing's Wrong." I'll pout, whine, and otherwise make you and everyone around me miserable. You ask me what's wrong, and I say, "Nothing's wrong." You have to guess what's wrong.

Of course, what's wrong is that you didn't give me what I wanted in the first place. Because I wouldn't tell you what I wanted. Isn't this fun?

These games are like an old story called the Abilene Paradox. It's the story of a big family that piles into a car on a blistering hot day to drive into Abilene for ice cream. Nobody wants to go, but everyone assumes that everyone else wants to go. So, in the interest of being nice and not rocking the boat, they all do what not one of them really wants to do. Unfortunately, this happens in real life all too often. We do things that we don't want to do because we think that maybe the others want to do it and we're afraid to take a stand on something as potentially explosive as going for ice cream. Good grief!

Years ago, I was at a rock concert with three friends. The concert was awful. I was more than bored. I was miserable. As an act of great courage, I summoned all my will and strength and said, "I'm not having fun. Are you?" All three of them said, "No. Let's get out of here."

We split. We went to the Bluebird Cafe and heard a stellar performance by Dave Olney and the X-Rays. It was fabulous; we had a ball, and we would have missed it if somebody hadn't had the courage to say, "I'm not having fun. Are you?"

There is a ropes course in Nashville called Adventureworks. It's a series of obstacles and exercises that you do with others to learn about teamwork and communication. I was doing the course with a group of people, most of whom I didn't know. A wonderful woman named Sue Willard was my partner on an obstacle called the Wild Woozy. It involved each of us standing on thin cables opposite each other as we leaned forward in a precarious balancing act and made our way down the cable trying all the while not to fall. The key to making it through the obstacle was to maintain balance with your partner.

You soon discover that to get through the Wild Woozy you scream things at your partner like "Give it to me!!! Push harder!!! Put your weight into me!!!" It can sound really wild at times, but you're just trying to maintain balance and not fall. To do it successfully, you have to completely lean into the other person, and you especially have to communicate what you need from your partner.

"Give it to me." Bingo. Tell me what you want. Don't keep it a secret. If I am unable to give you what you want, well, we'll deal with that. But don't be dishonest or withhold the truth from me about what you want. It's not fair, and it doesn't work for either of us. It's bad business, and it's a ridiculous way to live.

22

I Said I Don't Know

Here's a test: What's going to happen next? As Mark Twain said, "I was gratified to be able to answer promptly. I said I don't know." Good answer. If you want to knock the blocks out from under someone's sense of well-being, just throw a little uncertainty at them. We hate not knowing what's going to happen next. Well, guess what. You *don't* know what's going to happen next. No one does. That information is not available. The question is can you be okay with that? This is the key to moving forward versus being frozen with uncertainty. We have to be able to embrace the unknown.

Think of the people that you work with. Who is the one that, when you throw him a curveball, a change of plans, or anything unexpected, throws his hands up in the air and goes into his patented "woe is me" rant?

"Well, this is just great," he'll say. "How do you expect me to do my job when you keep changing the rules on me? How am I supposed to hit my target numbers when you constantly pull the rug out from under me? When is somebody going to make up their mind around here and decide once and for all what we're doing and how we're supposed to do it?"

Never. There will never be one way to do it and "they" will never make up their mind because the marketplace, the customers, technology, the competition, and the world change every day. You don't create stability by not changing what you're doing. You create stability by being able to maintain your values while constantly changing to meet the needs of today, not yesterday.

Think, however, of a person that you work with who becomes the consummate show-off when confronted with changes. She adds the new changes to the 10 projects that she is already juggling and says, "Is that it? Is that all you've got for me today? Then get out of my way because I've got work to do." How valuable is that person to the team?

Here's the trick. It's not about knowing what's going to happen next. It's about being okay with knowing that whatever happens next, you can handle it. It's about being okay with the simple reality that you will never know what's going to happen next. That's the nature of life in today's world. We used to be able to predict the future much more accurately than we can today. It's not just that the changes we face are so dramatic; it's that they come at us so quickly and with so little advance warning.

It used to be that the way to succeed was to make the right choice. To succeed today means making the right choice, and then making the next right choice quickly enough. Regardless of what's going on in your world right now, get ready to switch gears. You may think you understand the situation, but the situation just changed. If you can't perform under those circumstances, then you have no place to go. In today's world, if you don't like the unknown, you're a fish that doesn't like water.

23

The Golden Circle
of Ignorance

When we start a job, a marriage, parenting, or any new endeavor, we start at the top of the Golden Circle of Ignorance. We are squarely on Ignorance. That simply means that we don't yet know what we're doing. We're not stupid, but we are ignorant. We simply haven't quite learned what's going on. As we gain experience, we move down the Golden Circle of Ignorance to the bottom, where we now are in the position of Expert. We are 10 feet tall and bulletproof. No one can tell us anything because we now know everything. We've been around the block enough times to have this thing down cold. We are invincible.

Then we get the blocks knocked out from under us a few times and we begin to wise up. We start to move up the other side of the Golden Circle of Ignorance until we get back where we started, squarely on Ignorance. But this time, it's a very self-aware and constructive version of Ignorance. Our attitude is that no matter how much experience we have or how much we think we know, we want to know more. We are open to new ways of doing everything. We are hungry to learn. The greatest lesson of experience is that there's always more to learn. When you make it back up to that point, it truly is golden.

Imagine what you might learn if you didn't already know it. Huh? Here's what I mean by that. We are incredibly limited by what we think we already know. If you want to experience true intellectual, creative, and even spiritual liberation, let go of preconceived notions, stereotypes, prejudices, and supposed facts that aren't facts at all. They're just assumptions.

It's tough to let go of what you think you know. But the payoff is incredible. Let go of what you think you know and you automatically see the world with new eyes. You become instantly more creative and a better problem solver. Letting go of preconceived notions can spark a new enthusiasm for everything in your life. Where you were once sure you didn't care for something, you now have to reevaluate the possibility that you might like it after all.

You never order the calamari because you know you don't like it. You know this in spite of the fact that you've never once tried it. Who knows? One bite might be all it takes to create a constant craving for calamari at every meal. And if that one bite confirms what you thought you knew all along (that you don't like it), then you've at least had the experience of making a decision based on something real rather than imagined.

Let go of the idea that you don't like something before you've even experienced it. It's utter liberation. This should include those things that you reject because of an experience that you had years ago. You might be missing out on the greatest thing ever and not even know it. The way to let go is simple. Just experience it again.

If you don't like jazz, then go to a jazz club. My wife didn't particularly like jazz until we heard Foreplay perform at the Blue Note in New York. Hearing and seeing jazz performed live changed her complete perception. When most people say, "No way," show-offs tend to say, "Why not?"

What's the worst that can happen? You might confirm that you really don't like what you thought you didn't like. Fine. Bravo. Victory. At least you're now making decisions and choices based on current information. The point is that things change. You change. Don't you want to find out what's changed about you? Aren't you even curious?

James Weinberg is my accountant. More important, he is my friend. One reason I value James's friendship is that he makes me think. He often comes at the world from a completely different perspective than I do. I find his opinions to be stimulating, especially when we disagree. If I find myself feeling intellectually stale, or even if I just want to think through my own opinion about a particular issue, I often go looking for James.

I find that for me to have confidence in my opinions it's extremely helpful to bounce them off people that I tend to disagree with. Or at least people that, like James, will challenge my thinking and help me to formulate ideas that make sense and are based on something more than a knee-jerk reaction to an issue or situation.

Here's a good rule to live by. If you haven't changed your opinion on a significant issue in the past few years, you might want to see your doctor for a check-up. It's possible that you're brain-dead. I find it fascinating that most people seem to be threatened by new ideas. New ideas don't scare me. I love them. I may end up disagreeing with them, but I love them. What scares me is the thought that I might become so attached to my old ideas that I stop thinking. If that happens, just take me out and shoot me. Life without thinking isn't worth living.

You don't have to choose between having strong core beliefs and being open to differing points of view. As a matter of fact, the stronger my core values and beliefs, the less threatened I am by differing points of view. I know who I am therefore I am anxious to listen to and talk with people who disagree with me. There's no threat. And I might learn something. One of my favorite experiences is to listen to someone who has a completely different view of the world than me and have that completely energizing experience of "Wow. I never thought of it that way." If I can let go of defending my own entrenched opinion long enough to listen to another viewpoint, I might actually learn something.

Thomas Jefferson said, "I tolerate with utmost latitude the right of others to differ from me in opinion." I have politically liberal friends who would never in a million years listen to someone like conservative radio personality Rush Limbaugh. And I know Rush Limbaugh devotees who would not in their lifetime ever dare to read a book written by a liberal. And yet these same people will often comment endlessly and with great authority about how wrong the other side is. It's laughable because they literally don't know what they're talking about.

How can you claim to respond intelligently to someone whose ideas you have never heard or read? Maybe it's my experience as a high school and college debater that makes me open to hearing the other side. In competitive debate, you take one side of an issue, then, in the next round, you take the other side. You must learn to see and defend both sides to be effective. This kind of training doesn't make you wishy-washy in your opinions. On the contrary, it gives you strength in what you believe because you've examined the issue from all sides.

Even if you have no desire to learn from other viewpoints, wouldn't you at least want to know what you're against? How can you think or talk intelligently about the world if you refuse to even look at half of it? Small minds are deathly afraid of exposure to what they think they disagree with. They can't let go of their unwillingness to hear the other side because, deep down, they are so afraid that they might discover that their mind might change even a little bit.

The more I learn from other points of view, the better I am able to continue to build a strong foundation of my own thinking because I've got more information with which to build. If I'm a conservative and I strongly disagree with, for example, a liberal writer on healthcare issues, it will be because I read his book on healthcare and I disagree with it. It won't be because some conservative political pundit told me to disagree with it.

The same holds true in the other direction. If I think a conservative presidential candidate is an idiot, it's because I've listened to what she has to say and I think it's goofy, not because some liberal editorial writer told me what to think.

It's been said that only fools and dead men don't change their minds. Try letting go of what you think you know. Think for yourself. Read the other side. Come from knowledge and experience, not assumptions. Aspire to reach that top position on the Golden Circle of Ignorance. Show-offs are curious. Show-offs always want to learn more.

24

What Have You Done for Me Next?

The big question in business used to be "What have you done for me lately?" Today, we're not so interested in what happened "lately" anymore. Today, we're interested in what happens next. We have truly become an "I want it yesterday" society, and we have no patience for what we judge to be unnecessary waiting. If you make me wait, you lose.

So you'll get back with me tomorrow? Great. That gives me lots of time to find somebody else to do business with because you're fired. Believe it or not, I still run into people who take great chest-swelling pride in their policy of returning calls within 24 hours. Wake up and smell the millennium, folks. It's the twenty-first century, not the nineteenth. While you're looking at your calendar to find a time to get back to your customers, they're looking at their watches.

I've been a quick responder for so long that I've built it into my DNA. It's probably the simplest version of showing off that I know, and the payoff is amazing. My rule of thumb is that anything involving human contact should be done as quickly as possible. That includes returning phone calls, responding to emails, RSVPing to invitations, sending thank you letters, and anything else that will cause a living, breathing human being to say, "Dang. That guy is good."

I am a fan of NetFlix, the movie rental company that sends DVDs by mail. Here's what knocks me out about NetFlix. I get a DVD, watch it, and then put it in the mail to return. The next day, I get an email from NetFlix saying that they've received the DVD, and that the next one on my list is being sent to me immediately. The following day, I get the new DVD. How does NetFlix get the U.S. Postal Service to operate at lightning speed? What's the secret code? I am knocked out at the speed and efficiency at which this company operates. They are such complete show-offs.

In business, being known for a quick response can do wonders for your reputation. By contrast, if you make people wait, then you've committed the unforgivable sin in a world that wants it yesterday. Think about your own reaction to waiting. We hate to wait. We feel belittled and taken advantage of when we're made to wait. We will fire companies that make us wait, and we'll talk trash about them to everybody we know.

If you're in a situation beyond your control that dictates you must make someone wait, then at the very least you should acknowledge it. I've sent short emails explaining that I am completely tied up right now but that I will send a more complete email as soon as it is humanly possible. Simply acknowledge the other person. It's done nothing but score points for me with the people I do business with. The same thing goes for phone calls. I'll return a call and say, "Hey, I'm in a meeting and can't talk now, but we'll be breaking up later this afternoon and I'll call you then." It's magic. I can't stress enough the business or career-building power of having people regularly say to you, "Wow. I really appreciate how quickly you got back to me."

Let's not even begin to get into the whole subject of breaking time-based promises. It's one thing to be late with your response, delivery, or whatever, but if you've told me that it will be done on Monday and by Wednesday I'm still waiting, then you're on your way to becoming history with me. If there's a delay, tell me. Just tell me what's going on and the chances are that all will be forgiven.

On a personal level, there's probably nothing more disrespectful than being chronically late or making people wait. You're sending a message that says, "Your time means nothing to me. Your time is worthless. Therefore, you are worthless." Being chronically late is something that I am incapable of understanding. I don't get it. I can see getting unexpectedly caught in traffic once in a blue moon, but I simply don't understand being late over and over. And now you're thinking, "He must not have kids." Wrong. We've got two little girls. And if I say I'll meet you at 7:00, then I'll meet you at 7:00. Start getting ready earlier. Leave earlier. Or stop promising that you'll be there at 7:00 when you know good and well that it's not possible for you to be there until 8:00. Holy cow! Is this rocket science? What part of this would someone conceivably not understand?

If you take one idea from this book, I'm happy if it's this one. Be quick. Do it now. Be on time. Keep your promises.

25

The Power Strategy

What misguided thinking it is to believe that taking responsibility means taking the blame. What taking responsibility does is give you power. It maximizes your power. It creates power where otherwise you would have none. If you own it, you control it. To the extent that you make someone else responsible, you put that person in charge of your life.

Consider the following exchange:

My boss treats me badly.
What are you going to do about it?

But I'm not doing anything wrong. It's my boss. She's mean and unfair.
What are you going to do about it?

And that's not all. My best friend lied to me.
What are you going to do about it?

He really hurt my feelings.
What are you going to do about it?

But wait, it gets worse.
I'm sure it does.

I'm getting ripped off by big business.
What are you going to do about it?

The river in our town is polluted.
What are you going to do about it?

My boyfriend treats me like dirt.
What are you going to do about it?

Poor people are being treated unfairly by the system.
What are you going to do about it?

I'm planning to go to the lake this weekend and now
it's supposed to rain.
What are you going to do about it?

My hair is falling out.
What are you going to do about it?

My job stinks.
What are you going to do about it?

I'm bored with my lousy life.
What are you going to do about it?

You sound like a broken record. None of this is my
fault! I shouldn't have to do anything about it.
*You probably shouldn't. And that has absolutely nothing
to do with anything. Now. What . . . are . . . you . . .
going . . . to . . . do . . . about . . . it?*

I'm not going to do anything about it! It's NOT MY
   FAULT!

*Here's the problem with your strategy of not doing any-
   thing about it—it won't work. What part of that do
   you not understand? It won't work. You won't get
   what you want. It doesn't matter that you shouldn't
   have to do anything about it. It doesn't matter that
   it's not your fault. Not doing anything about it will
   not work.*

Then I guess I'll just be miserable because I'm not
   going to do anything about it.

Your call. Your choice

If your strategy is to make your life someone else's responsibility, I advise you to change strategies at once.
Putting other people in charge of your life is not exactly a
power strategy. It won't work. Period. It's a stupid strategy
that gives all of your power to someone else.

Here's the power strategy: It's my life. I did it. I made
the choices. I own it.

I had to let go of thinking that what happened in my
life was someone else's job or someone else's choice. It
was always my choice. If I lay claim to that responsibility
then I'm in charge. So who's in charge of your life? You
or somebody else? Decide. If you've made your life somebody else's job, then you need to fire them from that position and take on the job yourself. It's liberation day.

26

Your Next Best Idea
Is Everywhere

If you're looking for the next big idea for your business or career, go to the mall. Or you could go to an office building, a college campus, a church, a hockey game, a car wash, a museum, a state fair, or anywhere else. Incredible ideas can inspire you are everywhere. I mean that quite literally. You are surrounded by amazing, simple, adaptable ideas that can change your business or your life. If you just keep your eyes and mind open, you'll discover that virtually every place is an idea factory. Your next best idea is everywhere.

For example, here's a hot new idea from the mall. There's a new trend sweeping store design these days, especially in upscale malls. What I love about the idea behind this trend is that it runs so counter to the traditional wisdom about what works in retail sales. I love any idea that flies in the face of what everybody thinks is the only way to do something. The very best and most effective ideas are often counterintuitive.

The hot new idea is that you take the windows out of the front of the store and wall it up. That's right. The big windows that display the store's merchandise are bricked up and you close off everything from the view of your potential shoppers. Madness? Maybe not.

The reason that closing off your business to shoppers works for some stores—in spite of the fact that it seems completely illogical—is that it creates an aura of exclusivity. You don't go in the store unless you're in the know. It's cool. It creates a certain mystique. You have to be hip enough to know what's in there or adventurous enough to walk in without knowing what's in there in order to qualify as a customer. It works particularly well with the upscale teen market.

The practical lesson for me, and for my fellow show-offs, is that I should consider the power of mystique in my own business. Perhaps rather than try to appeal to the broadest market segment possible, I should narrow my focus and position myself to dominate in a very narrow niche.

Show-offs have their antennae out for new ideas all the time. They are constantly looking for what's going on in other businesses or endeavors that can inspire progress or improvement in their own lives and work. The key is to understand the power of adaptive innovation. Great ideas seldom, if ever, spring up from nothing. The best ideas usually come from seeing what works in one arena, then transferring it to a completely different arena.

In other words, innovation is most decidedly not rocket science. Innovation is a matter of seeing something that works and saying, "Hey, I could do that." Duh. This is why some makers of luxury automobiles send everyone from designers to sales consultants to visit Tiffany's, Four Seasons Hotels, and five-star restaurants. The idea is to see what those guys are doing that we should be doing. Of course, you have to be creative enough to translate a great idea from extraordinary service in a restaurant to the selling process in the car business, but that's a skill that comes from practice.

As an exercise in showing off and adaptive innovation, I took a field trip to my local shopping mall for a morning. My goal was to find 10 ideas that could be transferred to virtually any business. I went in search of inspiration—which is easy to find if you are a dedicated and practiced show-off. Here are the ideas that I found.

Idea 1: *Ask for the business.*

Idea 2: *Be sure the customer knows everything you've got to offer.*

When I placed my order for a grande nonfat latte and a *New York Times*, the Starbucks employee pointed out a pastry in the display case. "You've got to try this," she said, pointing to a new pastry item. "Why should I?" I asked. "Because it's incredible," she said. I bought it. It was incredible.

Two ideas are screaming out of this transaction and they are both excruciatingly obvious and painfully simple. The first idea is to ask for the business. If you simply come right out and ask people for their business, it's amazing how often they'll say yes. The single greatest failing of many businesses is that they just don't ask enough people to buy their stuff. Strange but true.

The second idea from this Starbucks transaction is to be sure that your customer, your boss, or whomever it may be that you're trying to impress, knows the full range of what it is that you've got to offer. If you've got a pastry that is "incredible," then say so, and say it often. Don't keep it a secret.

Idea 3: *How can you add value by taking something away?*

As I enjoyed my latte, incredible pastry, and the *New York Times*, idea number 3 slapped me across the brain. An advertisement for Chase Bank in the newspaper stated, "Bookkeeping is simpler when there aren't any books." The ad was about a bank program that lets your accountant or bookkeeper have access to your account records. Idea number 3 is that I should consider how I can make my customer's life easier by taking some burden or chore away. How can I add value by eliminating something? Chase Bank took away the books. Soft drink 7-UP built a brand by being the Uncola. They took away the color and the caffeine. What can you take away?

Idea 4: *Go where the competition isn't.*

I left Starbucks and began my stroll through the mall. In the middle of the mall floor, sitting right outside the doors of the Bebe, Sharper Image, Coach, J. Crew,

and Talbot's Woman stores, was a bright red, Jaguar X
Type 3.0. The lesson was obvious. Go where the competition isn't. If that Jaguar had been in the middle of
twenty other luxury cars, I wouldn't have noticed it.
What worked was that it was out of place. Instead of always going head to head with your competition, go
someplace unexpected where you'll stand out.

Idea 5: *Be functional.*

Just down the mall floor from the Jaguar, the same
auto dealer had placed an Audi. This time the lesson was
on the advertising poster next to the car. It read "Functional can be elegant." Whack! The greatest luxury is
something that works. Are you too focused on coming up
with buzzers and bells for what you offer that you miss
the power of simply offering something that works extremely well?

Idea 6: *Find your niche.*

Lady Footlocker store. Need I say more? It's a store
that focuses on a narrow product line to a particular market niche. Sell sports shoes and clothing to women who exercise. Don't say, "We've got shoes for everyone!" Say,
"We've got the right shoe for a particular group of people."
Those particular people will beat a path to your door.

Idea 7: *Hanging out.*

As I strolled through the mall, I couldn't help but notice all of the people who were walking for exercise.
There's a whole community of people who go to malls
early, before the stores actually open, and walk themselves silly. It's a great place to exercise and socialize and

it made me wonder, "Do I create community with my business?"

The idea can apply to an individual as well as a company. It comes down to your ability to create connections between people. The mall does it by providing a place for people to walk. You might do it by being a person who organizes social events, or who is the local "expert" on new movies that come out, or who knows the coolest restaurants in town. What makes you a magnet for people?

An Infiniti dealer in St. Louis focuses on being a destination, not just for car buying, but for classes and special events. He wants his car dealership to be seen as a hub of activity that brings people together from the community. More and more businesses understand the marketing power of being seen as a place that connects people, rather than just a store or office building.

Idea 8: *Mesmerize.*

As I passed the Aveda store, I was drawn to the compelling advertising display that had just one word written on it: "Mesmerize." I immediately considered whether or not I spend too much time talking about the features of what I offer, rather than getting straight to what my customer is really interested in—what it does for them. The fact is that most customers couldn't care less "how" you do what you do, they just want to know what the result is.

Whether you're offering a service or applying for a job, think in terms of pointing out all of the grand and glorious things that will happen when people do business with you or hire you. The Aveda store wasn't advertising a list of ingredients that they use in their products. They were selling the benefit of what happens when you use those products. You will "mesmerize." And who doesn't want to mesmerize?

Idea 9: *Teach people how and why to love you.*

The Williams Sonoma cookware store was offering classes on how to make homemade relish for Thanksgiving. It's a no-brainer. To sell more cooking stuff, teach people how to cook. Do you teach your customers to get maximum value from what you sell? The more people know about how wonderful you and your products or services are, the more they'll want.

My wife recently bought a new camera. For the first time ever with a camera, she dove into the instructions on how to use and get the most out of it. A funny thing happened. The more she learned about how to use the camera, the more she loved it. For the first time, she is actually enthusiastic about a camera.

I know that I'm guilty of not always helping my customers know how to get the most out of what I can do for them. It's not their job to know how or why to hire me. It's my job to be sure that I've taught them all the reasons to do so.

Idea 10: *Give it away.*

The Kiehl's since 1851 skin care products store gives away free samples of almost everything they sell. Again, we're in no-brainer territory. If you've got something of value, give it to people; they'll love it, then they'll buy it.

That's exactly what Debbie Fields did when she started Mrs. Field's Cookies. She'd bake a batch of cookies, take them outside the store, and give them to people passing by. The rest is cookie history. What this idea means to me is that if I have a talent or skill that I feel has value, I try it out with people for free. If it, in fact, has value, the marketplace will create demand for it.

Idea 11: *Less is more.*

As I passed by Tiffany's jewelry store, I noticed that they seemed to have less on display than any other jewelry store in the mall. Sometimes, less really is more. Too many choices can freeze people into indecision. Too much to choose from can obscure. Less can reveal.

I've seen people in the professional speaking business offer 10 or more topics that they claim to be an expert in, from time management and sales to leadership and team building. I've seen resumes do the same thing. If you claim to be all things, the obvious conclusion that people will reach is that you're probably not very good at anything. What is your true strength? Go with that.

Idea 12: *Be easy to do business with.*

The Apple computer store devoted much of its display space to the iPod. I don't blame them. The iPod is one of the most remarkable and best-selling products in recent history. One of the great product strengths of the iPod is that it's easy to use.

So what does an easy-to-use iPod have to do with me? Everything. What I have to ask myself is whether or not I am "easy to use" and do business with? Am I easy to negotiate with, work with, or be on a team with? If I make it hard to do business with me, the marketplace will replace me in a heartbeat. If I'm the employee that's hard for everyone to get along with, then I've sabotaged my own career. There are too many talented people out there for anyone to put up with a jerk for long. I need to be like the iPod. I need to be "user-friendly" and easy to do business with.

My stroll in the mall in search of 10 ideas exceeded the goal. I got 12, and I didn't even work up a sweat. I just noted the incredibly obvious. Showing off requires the ability to see an idea and let it be the catalyst that inspires you to transfer it to your world. Become a master of adaptive innovation and you will be able to continuously improve and constantly innovate in whatever you do.

27

What Matters Most

What matters most to you? What's truly important in your life? There's no right or wrong answer to that question. I'm not here to make a judgment on what should be important to you. What counts is whether or not your answer is in alignment with your actions. If it isn't, then you're living in conflict. Without getting too "out there," let me suggest that if your actions are out of alignment with what you claim is important to you, you're heading for a train wreck. I speak to you from experience. Been there. Done that.

I know people in my line of work who, when asked what's most important in their lives, will respond with great feeling and conviction that family and friends are what they hold to be most dear. "It's all about people, my friend. It's all about the love," they'll say. Then they rush to the airport to get on the next plane that will take them away from family and friends so that they can pursue what is really important to them—making more money.

What's wrong with this picture isn't the pursuit of money. If buying more stuff is what floats their boat, then that's their call. What's wrong with this picture is that they are living a lie. If money is what drives you, then just say so—get your values in alignment with your actions and eliminate the inner battle that's working against you and probably stressing you out. You'll probably make even more money and you won't have that pesky conflict of what you say versus what you do.

Some will read this and raise an impassioned defense along the lines of "It's not the money! I pursue the money for the security and well-being of my family! I take offense, sir, at your accusation!" Yeah, fine. If you have to work two jobs to make enough to feed your family, then I'm not talking about you. That's called doing the right thing. I'm talking about those who have more money than they need, but can't quit the drug. I'm talking about what can happen with a lack of clarity and alignment between actions and declared values.

I think a great case can also be made that those who live their lives in alignment with their values do, in fact, achieve a greater degree of success over the long run. I believe that if you forget about the money, you'll probably make more money. Do the right thing and the windows of prosperity will open and pour riches unimagined throughout your life. That's not wishful thinking. That's the way it works.

I have a friend who recently retired as CEO of a very successful company. He was a dynamo in his career. He achieved remarkable financial success and retired as a respected and beloved leader with a legacy of noteworthy achievement in business. Throughout his life and career, there was never a doubt about what came first with him. At the top of the list were his family and his faith, and they weren't up for debate. He would skip a company meeting to be with his daughter on her birthday. He would turn down a lucrative contract because something about it didn't line up with his sense of values. He found the greatest joy not in the art of the deal, but in the joy of being with family and friends.

He lived by the philosophy: "Do the right thing and the money will take care of itself." He is now retired and is financially set. He could live anywhere in the world. He could be pursuing a never-ending string of luxury cruises and resort vacations. Where you will find him is reading to kids at a family center located in an inner-city housing project, putting together a fund-raiser to support the work of that center, working in his church, or otherwise helping make the world a better place.

I believe with all of my heart and mind that what made this guy such a remarkable success is that he had a foundation that was rock solid. He had a compass that always pointed true north. Because he knew what was truly important to him throughout his career, he was able to build something of value to himself and others. Along the way, there were undoubtedly some who perceived him as not having the "right stuff" to successfully climb the corporate ladder. He didn't have a killer instinct. What he did have, that ultimately put him on top of that corporate ladder, was integrity and clarity about his values.

Look at companies with long records of stability and success. You'll find that virtually all of them have a very strong sense of values and culture. They're able to make decisions and take action more effectively than their competitors because they know who they are. That success flows directly from culture.

Most companies talk a great game when it comes to their culture. They've got a mission statement, a vision statement, and a values statement—all of which are the subject of great attention at the annual company meeting. Then these various statements are put back in the bottom of somebody's desk drawer to sleep peacefully until next year's meeting.

It's not easy for a business or an individual to formulate a true statement of what's important, much less to live by it. You have to let go of the luxury of being lazy. It takes time and energy to work at developing and living by a clear, strong set of values. You have to clear the space to let those values take hold. But the payoff is considerable.

Certain companies and individuals have a predisposition to high performance. It's in their DNA. It's in the air that they breathe. Those companies and people are the ones that work at culture every day. It's not a part-time endeavor. It's a critically important part of what they do all day long. Who they are is as important as what they do.

Every action they take is driven by this heightened sense of culture, values, and identity. This isn't about having a "feel good" mission statement. This is about what drives your strategies and execution.

It's important to build emotion into your mission. Reverend Martin Luther King Jr. didn't say, "I have a strategic plan." Make no mistake about it, Reverend King most certainly had a strategic plan. But what he's remembered for, and what drove him and eventually millions of people to stand up for the cause of civil rights, were the words: "I have a dream."

In business, we often make the fundamental mistake of thinking that for an idea to be professional, it's got to be devoid of emotion. Nothing could be further from the truth. An idea is only truly professional if it works, and what works is to connect with emotion. Connect with the heart and the mind will follow. Whether it's your own personal mission statement or that of your business, don't water it down into some empty, vanilla blob of meaningless corporate-speak. Say something with some guts in it. Say something that will make you stand up taller and take a deep breath of pride. Say something that gives you goose bumps.

Companies that are daily guided by their values are no different than the person who begins each day with prayer, meditation, or affirmations. If you are grounded in what's important, then you can act decisively. As unexpected challenges and opportunities come up, you act based on the sure strength of knowing what's important.

If you haven't created your own personal mission statement, get started. It's the basis for a successful life. Get clarity on what matters most. Remember that if you feel strongly about what you do, use strong language. Say something with some substance to it.

> We're on a mission from God.
> —The Blues Brothers